DEATH
Takes TIME

"Dr. Baillie has given us a realistic book about life and death. It will comfort many and sober up some."
— Michael Youssef, PhD, Founding Pastor
Church of the Apostles, Atlanta, GA
Author of *The Leadership Style of Jesus*

"I have read *Death Takes Time*. Thank you, Gene Baillie, for sharing it with me. You've done a great job of dealing opening and honestly with the subject of death, a subject about which most Americans are very uncomfortable.

"You've used Scripture well, weaving it throughout your personal reflections as well as practical lessons related to one dying. I especially like the end of the book, when you delineate the step-by-step process required following death (as well as the admonition to be prepared well in advance, as much as is possible).

"You beautifully communicate the privilege you had to walk with your beloved 'til the end. In a culture that is so convenience oriented, you paint a sweet picture of letting go of your own propensity to control and submitting to the sovereign God who *is* in control.

"From a very personal and honest position, Dr. Gene Baillie invites us to examine our understanding of death as a process, not an event. Rich in scriptural truth and poignant in personal testimony,

Death Takes Time is a helpful read for anyone, but especially for those whose end is in view and for those walking with them."
— Dr. Virginia Friesen, Co-Director
Home Improvement Ministries
www.HIMweb.org
Author of *Raising a Trailblazer: Rite-of-Passage Trail Markers for Your Set-Apart Teen* and co-author of *The Marriage App*

"As I reviewed this book for my dad, I see how it ministers to those who are in the midst of raw and hurting emotions as they respond to the death of a loved one, at first only possible in a superficial way. But, so much more, the book also ministers to the needs of dealing with the physical and spiritual depth of ongoing grief.

"There are the practical lists of things to be done but also the strong message of the presence of a loving God to minister through His Word, prayer, plus the wonderful privilege of other believers coming alongside in your time of need, loving and strengthening one another.

"And, throughout is the strong reminder to use wisely the time the Lord allows us on this earth, time He uses for our good, our ministry, and for His glory."
— Rebecca A. Baucum, RN
Greenville, SC

DEATH
Takes TIME
Make the Best Use of Your Time

Dr. Gene Baillie

Cover design by Diana Lawrence
Interior design and e-book by Lisa Parnell

ISBN 978-0-996497-22-0 (print)
ISBN 978-0-9964972-3-7 (e-book)

Printed in United States of America

22 21 20 19 18 17 16   1 2 3 4 5

THIS BOOK IS DEDICATED TO ...

My God, Provider of my time and my every breath. He created this world and placed me in this life at the moment He desired, allowing every continuing second for my good and His glory.

The "wife of my life," Gini, my companion during our earthly journey for fifty-one and a half years.

And to our daughters, Becky, Kim, and Heather; our foster sons, Nathan, Wesley, Brian, and Travis; and our many spiritual children, all our grandchildren, and generations yet to come—that the Lord might not only continue to call them all to be His children, but that He might in some way use these written words to partially accomplish His perfect work in their lives.

Contents

Acknowledgments

I want to thank and praise God for giving me the ability and clarity to write the important truths contained in this book. He created the universe and all that is in it. He created time, He is light for the path we walk, He adopted us into His family for all eternity, and He gave us His Word with promises and provision for our daily needs. His provision also included conquering death.

During our time as aliens and strangers on this earth, we have been the recipients of God's grace and direction for each step we take. While we follow His leading and know He is holding our hands, we gratefully acknowledge He has given us all things—our souls and bodies, life and breath, worldly abilities, and provision for our needs, as well as saving faith to acknowledge Him as Savior, Lord, and Treasure. As we give Him glory and honor, may we never lose sight of knowing what He has begun in us He will complete according to His plan and in His perfect timing.

My wife Gini died of her brain cancer in May 2015. This book is published on the first anniversary of her death. What a life together for fifty-one and a half years! She was a helpmate in the truest sense. She was a godly wife, companion, counselor, mother, grandmother, and Bible teacher to children and women. Her life verse was 3 John 1:4: "I have no greater joy than this, to hear of my children [and she would add grandchildren, foster children, and spiritual children and grandchildren] walking in the truth." I praise God for the time we had together on this earth and the hope of spending eternity together, with all the family of our Lord, as we give praise and glory to Him. (If you are curious about this book's cover, which resembles our front yard, pp. 53–54 and the opening quote on p. 59 explain it.)

Sarah Arndt, a friend and excellent writer, helped me greatly! She spent many hours at the computer, went through many critiques, and took my notes and organized the first draft of this book. Gary Terashita provided additional editing, followed by excellent copyediting and layout by Lisa Parnell. I am appreciative of the cover design by Diana Lawrence.

I also thank Michael Youssef, Virginia Friesen, Scott Anderson, Chase Marshburn, John Boyte, Katherine Swathwood, Dale Treash, and Elsie Newell for reviewing, editing, and helpful comments as well as encouragement.

A Message to Readers

*"I thought I could describe a state;
make a map of sorrow. Sorrow, however,
turns out to be not a state but a process."*[1]

— C.S. LEWIS

It was the largest and bloodiest battle the United States faced in the Second World War. The Battle of the Bulge, lasting for more than a month, resulted in nearly 80,000 American soldier casualties. One of those soldiers, my uncle Elwood, was only twenty years old. He entered the army six weeks before his death and spent just three days in Europe before the Germans' surprise attack. At the time of his funeral four years later, I was only six years old, but I still remember the rifle salute ringing out over his gravesite.

As a toddler when he left for the front, I have no memory of Uncle Elwood except a modest collection of used stamps kept in a small spiral-bound notebook I received after his death. The lack of time spent with my uncle Elwood is in steep contrast to

the time I spent with my mother's two other brothers, one of whom is alive and in his nineties at the
time of this writing. In a recent conversation with
my mother (she was the oldest and Elwood the
second child), she commented on his death, "I had
many memories of my brother, but realized I'd never
get to see him again on this earth."

The seemingly unfortunate timing of my uncle's early death occurring when I was only a child,
vague memories enhanced only by frayed stamps
and loud guns—what relationship could have
formed between the two of us had death not taken
the time away? A healthy, strong twenty-year-old
man is supposed to have decades left, but his time
was snatched away as quickly as a bullet buzzes
by an ear. Death also denied time from the other
soldiers killed in that battle as well as from their
families. Indeed death has denied time in various
ways for billions of people over thousands of years.

A little more than seventy years after the un-
timely death of my young uncle, I have now experienced a different kind of death, the type of death
that takes time in a whole new sense. I was married
to Gini for fifty-plus years. She developed a brain
tumor four years before I started working on this
book. She lived much longer than the statistics pre-
saged, although we were told in the spring of 2011

the glioblastoma would take the "wife of my life" in a matter of months. Four years later, I felt ready to reflect on the juxtaposition of the grief felt when we first got the news of cancer with the resulting joy the Lord brought both of us by allowing us the additional time during her gradual declining journey toward physical death.

The length of Gini's illness gave us much more time together than expected, but it also took from us so much time in the process. From long car rides to Duke to what felt like even longer periods in the doctor's office waiting room, Gini's journey toward death took time from her, from me, and even from others. However, I do not think it would have been any easier had Gini's death come suddenly. Either way, her death removed any additional time together on this earth.

The Lord has ordained each of our days and our time on the earth, and the days Gini and I had together prepared our eternal perspectives. As I reflect on what death has taught me about time and on what time has taught me about death, the one main conclusion I come to is death—whether it is the kind that comes to a young soldier on a chaotic battlefield or the kind that comes in the quietness of a hospital bed in our home—always takes time.

Gini went home to be with her Lord on May 21, 2015; death ended her time on this earth.

I have used the statement "death takes time" not only for my title but also several times in this preface. Now is a good opportunity to make sure the reader does not think I am giving death any power or ability to do anything. That is not the aim of this book. As I reflect on death, including Gini's, and consider my own future, I realize that by saying death is taking time, I am giving to it a power it simply does not have. Death does not have the power or ability to take away our time! However, when death occurs or is delayed, we tend to have thoughts similar to the title of this book with its concept and the play on words.

"There is a time for everything, and a season for every activity under the heavens: a time to be born and a time to die."
— ECCLESIASTES 3:1–2A (NIV)

Though, as each second passes, it may seem death has taken at least one more second to occur, and though no more earthly seconds remain in our life when death does occur, God is in charge of the seconds of our lives. Though it seems death is *taking* in both instances, God is in charge and the Victor! Only God is the Creator and Giver of what we consider our time. He also numbers our seconds and directs the use of time. At death, our earthly time has ended. But death is an event, not a presence or a power able to do anything.

Be careful not to fall into a false thinking trap. Death does not have the power to take life any more than to steal time! Death appears to take time in both senses I am writing about, but death has been swallowed up in the victory of our risen Lord, death has lost its sting, death has no power, death has no control, death is but a shadow as we pass from life to life!

As we live on this earth and our allotted future time diminishes, I believe the Lord has given us the ability to more clearly understand the coming future day of our own death when we will have no more earthly time. Our focus will be totally eternal, outside the bounds of earthly time.

The goal of this book and counsel to readers is to acknowledge time is passing moment by moment and to properly use the time you have left on this earth. I want you to know death will end your time on this earth so, in that sense, death takes time. I also want you to know each day you remain, your life has been prolonged another day, the other sense of death taking time.

I know I am going to die if the Lord does not return first. I have watched the process intimately, and I have no need to dwell on or fear death; I am to simply follow the Lord for the proper use of the remainder of my days. I can confidently rest and trust in Him, and I have peace in His perfect plan.

May you be blessed in your reading to become the exact blessing to others the Lord intends with the time He has given to you on this earth. May you understand more fully how each second counts for eternity, but more importantly how you will use your time to finish well the perfect plan the Lord has prepared for you.

"You turn people back to dust, saying,
'Return to dust, you mortals.' A thousand years
in your sight are like a day that has just gone by,
or like a watch in the night. Yet you sweep people
away in the sleep of death—they are like the new
grass of the morning: In the morning it springs up
new, but by evening it is dry and withered."

— *PSALM 90:3–6 (NIV)*

CHAPTER 1

A Relative Exactness

"When you are courting a nice girl,
an hour seems like a second.
When you sit on a red-hot cinder,
a second seems like an hour.
That's relativity."[2]

— ALBERT EINSTEIN

"You're as slow as Christmas!" I am sure you can relate to this expression. For children, waiting for the arrival of Christmas Day is a true test of patience. Technically, Christmas Day comes at exactly one-year intervals. It is as precise as any measure of time. But, even that month-long period between Thanksgiving and Christmas Eve, for a young child, can seem like a lifetime. In fact, to them, it is much closer to a lifetime than for adults.

For instance, a four-year-old girl has lived a grand total of forty-eight months, so the month of anticipation between Thanksgiving and Christmas is a significant portion (2 percent) of her short life—and to wait for her next birthday is 25 percent of her life! On the other hand, a seventy-year-old man has lived 840 months, making a month seem like a blink (1/10th of 1 percent) of his lifetime. For him, there is barely time to take down the lights and wreaths before it is the next year and the time comes to put them up again! Even though the passage of the time is technically (exactly) the same, it is amazing how a difference in perspective can make it seem drastically longer or so much shorter.

> We are always living in the present, but we are not ever-present or omnipresent like God.

I am frequently intrigued by the idea that time is both relative and exact. Our days are often ruled by the precise measure of time, sometimes down to a few seconds. A constant watching of the time is necessary to prevent missing an activity, appointment, or even a favorite television show (fortunately, our digital age now allows us to record or watch at our leisure). Although everyone knows the incremental passage of time does not change, no one could deny that the more time one spends on the earth, the faster it seems to move.

For example, on my birthday nearly thirty years ago, someone asked how old I was turning.

Without a second thought, I quickly replied forty-three. As the friend offered her congratulations and left, I did the math and was mortified to realize I was not forty-three but actually forty-four!

Where had that year gone? Oh, by the way, in my mind right now, that birthday event seems just like yesterday.

Another example of both exact and relative in the same day is Easter. Each year we have the same Easter recurring as a specific remembrance of Christ's sacrificial death and resurrection on our behalf. But, besides being a set historical event on our calendars with yearly exactness, we know it does not occur on the same date each year. Its assigned day is relative to the position and cycle of the moon (the Sunday after the first full moon following the March equinox).

We are always living in the present, but we are not ever-present or omnipresent like God. Our future time is constantly disappearing as it becomes our present and then our past. In other words, today is always tomorrow's yesterday. This notion can be compared to water streaming over a cliff as a waterfall. The water once flowing downstream comes to the edge of the falls, but in an instant it becomes part of the pooling reservoir at the bottom. Our future time is always quickly going away (like water over the cliff), and at the same time, our past "pool" is ever increasing.

We often speak of this process as "running" out of time. This boggles our minds a bit for sure. As our allotted future time diminishes, I believe the Lord has given us the ability to more clearly understand the coming future day of our death when we will have no more earthly time and our focus will be totally eternal, outside the bounds of earthly time.

Psalm 90 tells the reader our days may come to seventy or eighty years. Before my wife, Gini, died at age seventy, she and I read through the Bible each year for more than twenty-five years—and we always paused at this psalm. Because the psalmist asks the Lord to teach us to number our days, Gini wrote a note in her Bible doing just that. She listed her remaining days in both 1991 and in 2002 if she were to live to seventy years. So, substituting the actual days for years (including leap year days) in this psalm, it would read, "As for the days of our life, they contain [25,567 days], or if due to strength, [29,220 days], yet their pride is but labor and sorrow; for soon it is gone and we fly away. . . . So teach us to number our days, that we may present to You a heart of wisdom" (90:10, 12 NASB).

Because every day has twenty-four hours, each with sixty minutes, that gives us 86,400 daily moments we call seconds. Therefore, a lifetime of eighty years gives you 2,524,608,000 seconds.

However, since Gini's brain cancer tumor progressed and her death occurred in her seventieth year, her life did not include 300 million of those seconds. Each day of our lives time has been used up or taken away, not to be available

"Teach us
to number our days,
that we may present
to You a heart
of wisdom."
— PSALM 90:12

again, and at death, our earthly time has ended (this is the proper way to think of death using up or taking away time). Each day of our lives death is using time to occur, yet death will take time away.

I understand the passage in Psalm 90 more clearly with every new day. I realize my perspective of time is changing. Now retired, I am no longer controlled as much by the clock in the sense of trying to make it to different appointments and activities on time. My schedule is no longer compartmentalized by the hour.

As a physician I was trained to determine whether a patient is "oriented as to person, place, and time." As I now reflect on how often I included such questions when assessing patients, I see this "disorientation" as a very real and completing part of end-of-life issues, aspects that often no longer matter. What I thought critical to correct, somehow is part of God's plan as the things of this earth grow progressively dim and we become more "oriented" and ready for our transfer to our heavenly home.

> Time matters less to us as we approach death because the Lord is preparing us for our release from this world's journey and its time.

In fact, in the last year of Gini's life it did not matter that she no longer had a concept of time. She did not know what day it was or even the year. She often did not know where we were going and dreamed of past events or thought she was back in her childhood home.

One morning in her last year, she finished breakfast and knew we would have physical therapy in the afternoon, but she also insisted I pack the suitcases for our trip to Nebraska, which was not planned for another few months. The closer she approached death, the more her perspective on time changed. I believe time matters less to us as we approach death because the Lord is preparing us for our release from this world's journey and its time.

First Corinthians 13:12 says, "For now we see in a mirror dimly, but then face to face. Now I know in part; then I shall know fully, even as I have been fully known." Even as the days seem long now, I know death is quickly approaching. With death impending, my eternal perspective is growing less and less dim, while the things of the world are slowly fading more and more into the shadows.

I think Gini's inadvertent merging of events of the past with those of the present foreshadows an eternal future without a sense of time, or at least time as we understand earthly time. On one hand, time has lost its significance as we wait for future glory, but, on the other hand, it has become so much more precious as we literally number the days we have left on earth.

"So we do not lose heart. Though our outer self is
wasting away, our inner self is being renewed day
by day. For this light momentary affliction
is preparing for us an eternal weight of glory
beyond all comparison, as we look not to the things
that are seen but to the things that are unseen.
For the things that are seen are transient,
but the things that are unseen are eternal."

— *2 CORINTHIANS 4:16–18*

CHAPTER 2

Some Ways Death Takes Time

"Death is like my car.
It takes me where I want to go."
— JOHN PIPER

We usually think of our lives moving toward eventual death as a downward spiral, but in fact it is better termed as an upward spiral toward life. Every day we live we are indeed losing another day of time on earth, but we are also one day closer to eternal life because death has lost its sting. Death only lasts for a moment before we enter eternal life, being more alive than we have ever been. Indeed, our earthly bodies are in a downward spiral of decay as we live out this earthly life. That is what we notice as we age, but as Christians we need to be aware of and concentrate on the reality of our spiritual lives.

When we die, our soul will immediately be in the presence of our Lord for all eternity, and we also know we then will have our promised new bodies.

Recently, I had a conversation with a friend whose husband lay dying in the ICU. Because they own a farm, the longer he remained in the ICU, the further their farm chores and responsibilities fell by the wayside. Many of their friends took time out of their schedules to make sure the animals on the farm were fed and watered. Moreover, my friend spent much of her time, normally filled with household and farm duties, worrying about her husband, visiting him in the ICU, and talking with the nurses and doctors. This example shows us an aspect of how death takes time from friends and family—both in time you cannot spend with them and the time they, as well as strangers, have taken to serve you.

As my wife progressed toward her death, it took her longer to do things, like chewing, swallowing, and standing up—activities that would take a healthy person so much less time. Her movements were slow and even less deliberate, taking more and more time from myself and certainly from other caregivers to feed, assist, and generally care for her needs. Keeping her stabilized to even take a few steps was only one of many daily tasks that became huge events, often requiring the assistance of more than one person. A meal could take up to two hours, so the caregiver or I had to juggle tasks a bit, trying to accomplish a few other things between bites!

When she could not talk except occasional words and several directed questions were required to obtain even a simple head nod, communicating also took additional time. If, after a few moments, we did not see a head nod, we then moved on to a second or third question to bring back her focus. Here is an example of a typical dialogue:

"Do you want toast and eggs?" No response.

"Do you want cereal?" No answer.

"Do you want only toast?"

Her head nodded slightly and her eyes brightened. Finally, success!

Another situation arose during Gini's illness. Through the years, she and I enjoyed taking our grandchildren on vacations and trips. But, during

"Then I will make up *[or restore]* to you for the years that the swarming locust has eaten, the creeping locust, the stripping locust and the gnawing locust, my great army which I sent among you."
— JOEL 2:25 (NASB, emphasis mine)

her four years of illness and decline, I faced a dilemma: should I take the grandchildren on trips and leave Gini behind as she previously instructed me to do, or should I put the trips on hold until after her death, losing some of the limited time I could spend with our growing grandchildren? On one hand, leaving Gini at home with someone else takes away the little time we had left together; but, on the other hand, giving up precious time I could spend with my grandchildren, some of whom live halfway across the country, was hard to swallow as well. In this situation, there is no clear or right answer, so even more time can be consumed dwelling on what to do (I took the grandchildren on trips and sent pictures nearly every day for family and caregivers to show to Gini).

"Happy Valentine's Day to my sweet dad! May the Lord give you a sweet day. I'm sure Mom will be on your mind a lot, as she always is. Thank you for giving us a legacy of an amazing marriage and such an intertwining of love and lives that we couldn't always tell you apart! . . . I love you, Dad."
— Kimberly Baillie Woodward, RN
Brentwood, Tennessee

Watching someone else die takes time away from other things and other people in life. As one grows older, funerals of close acquaintances become more and more frequent. Sometimes, these may seem like such a waste of time, not only for family and friends but even the time of police officers who provide assistance for the procession. We may feel we should have used the time to be at work or doing something else we consider far more important.

Recently, our pastor was called to give a message at the funeral of an extended family member. He considers it an honor and privilege to speak at funerals, especially because it gives him an opportunity to witness to those attendees who are not Christians. However, the request came midweek, along with all his other pastoral duties, like sermon preparation. Moreover, the service fell on the same day and same time as his four-year-old daughter's planned birthday party, which consequently had to be changed. Death took his time in so many ways, but in this instance, it took time from his family and pastoral duties, time only the Lord can fully restore.

Wakes and funerals often require traveling a long distance, meeting with the family, and supporting their grieving process. Funerals can truly seem like a waste of time, until you realize, in a sense, they are part of the preparation for your own death. I have had the experience of contemplating my own death at almost every funeral I have attended but quite vividly many years ago at my father's funeral.

The evening before, at visitation, an elderly farmer in my small hometown of twelve hundred, whom I had not seen in thirty years, came up to me and asked if I was Eugene. Surprised, I replied that I was, and after he confirmed I was the oldest child, he commented dryly, "Well, you are now at the head of the conveyor belt!" Despite his blunt farming jargon, I could not help but smile and ponder this great truth. Generations come and generations go; at some point I will be the next in line to depart this earth.

As I summarized in the Message to Readers section, my own death is approaching second by second. If I say death is taking my own time, I realize I am giving to death a power it simply does not have! Death does not have the power or ability to take away our time. However, when death occurs or is delayed, we tend to think of the title of this book, its concepts; and the play on words seems to catch our attention.

As each second passes, it may seem death has taken at least that one more second to occur; and though there are no more earthly seconds in our life when death does occur, God has been in charge of every second of our lives. Though it seems that death is taking in both instances, God is in charge and the Victor! Only God is the Creator and Giver of what we consider our time. He

> Death is an event, not a presence or a power that can do anything.

also numbers our seconds and directs the use of time. As stated earlier, each day of our lives results in time used up or taken away, not to be available again; and at death, our earthly time has ended. But death is an event, not a presence or a power that can do anything.

After considering all the thoughts and ideas of this chapter, plus many other memories of Gini and our fifty-one and a half years of married life together, it became ever clearer there was no better use of my time than to continue to be with and sit at the side of my dying wife, holding her hand, no matter how much time she "took." I also was privileged to take that time, and it was joyous. You see, "we were having the time of our lives."

My Car

When I arrived, I did not know it was my car,
Provided to me from afar,
Carefully cared for by Mom and Dad,
Not a single care I had.

In a car seat was my place,
Not even to walk, let alone race,
I was comfortable at home,
And had no reason to roam.

As I grew, I recognized the many cars around,
And soon took notice of my own in my surrounds,
I tentatively pushed on the gas pedal a time or two,
But was not to leave the garage with any of you.

As a teen I pushed on the limits of the gate,
And to drive along with Mom and Dad was first
    rate,
Then they let me drive alone,
With rules they taught me were to be my own,
I was allowed to test the road,
But not to be squished flat as a toad.

I then left that house and home,
To my own trail to now roam,
I planned my own journey for each day,
After a while sensed Another guiding my way.

I met a special car named Gini and together spent 51
    years,
Now two cars close, occasionally changing gears,
We sped up and down the highways,
Our journey took us on many byways,

We went and did and had so much fun,
All the time realizing there is nothing new under the
sun.

We spent time together reading the Guide's book,
Even teaching others young and old how to drive
and look,
We began to see our nothing was something,
Indeed, our own soul was that nothing.

Then one day her car began to slow and stall,
As she continued toward her upward call.
On the backstretch she was failing to keep up the
pace,
But said she had a helping Hand and would still
finish the race,

One day the car simply would not run,
I helped pull her aside and out of the fun and sun,
And soon in that same car in which she was born,
She gently was removed and not even torn,
I am certain her removal did not even hurt.
Now only an empty shell to return to dirt,
We both knew it was only a car on loan,
While on this earth's journey as an alien we did
roam.

My car too is no longer my own,
Mine too will run out of gas,
And beside the journey's path,
Will also decay in the grass,
My soul, too, will gently be removed,
As body and rim scatters,
May all see that her and my nothing matters.

— GENE BAILLIE

"O LORD, you have searched me and known me!
You know when I sit down and when I rise up;
you discern my thoughts from afar. You search out
my path and my lying down and are acquainted
with all my ways. Even before a word is on my
tongue, behold, O LORD, you know it altogether.
You hem me in, behind and before, and lay your
hand upon me. Such knowledge is too wonderful
for me; it is high; I cannot attain it."

— *PSALM 139:1–6*

CHAPTER 3

The God
of Time and Death

*"Someday, you will read in the papers that
D. L. Moody, of East Northfield, is dead. Don't you
believe a word of it! At that moment I shall be more
alive than I am now; I shall have gone up higher, that
is all, out of this old clay tenement into a house that
is immortal—a body that death cannot touch, that sin
cannot taint; a body fashioned like unto His glorious
body. I was born of the flesh in 1837. I was born of the
Spirit in 1856. That which is born of the flesh may die.
That which is born of the Spirit will live forever."[3]*

— DWIGHT L. MOODY (1837–99)

For many, the concepts of death and time, especially when considered together, are cause for much anxiety. Pondering these two ideas is worrisome because we as humans have no control or influence over either of them. We cannot change time, go back in time, or predict the future. We may also try very hard to prolong death by eating all the right things and exercising with the best fitness programs. But no matter how hard we try, we know in one way or another, death is coming.

One can have several responses to this inability to control our lives. Some may have attitudes that

Time is a gift and must be treated as such because it was never ours to begin with.

stem from a feeling of panic and fear, others from apathy or hopelessness. However, as Christian believers, when these feelings begin to fill our minds, we can find rest in the fact our lives are in the hands of a loving God who is sovereign over both death and time.

One of the reasons we know and trust God as sovereign over time is because He created it, and He is not bound by its limits or changed by its passing. He knows the beginning and the end. Although God is not confined by time, He chooses to work in time and sees across the sequences of world events. In orchestrating His perfect plan, God uses time as a tool to place certain events and people in particular order for His glory. Every second is under His control, along with every event that occurs in each particular second. Moreover, because God created and is sovereignly in control of time, it is His. Time belongs to God, not to us.

Flippantly, we may say things like, "You're wasting my time," or "I don't have time for this." Although statements like these frequent our thoughts and mouths, they are not really true. Any moment we are alive and active is not because we are entitled to it or have earned it. Rather, God truly gives us each moment. Time is a gift and must be treated as such because it was never ours to begin with. Time belongs to God, and this fact can give us much comfort when our time seems to be running short. It is good to remember time is not ours, and we must try to use any time we have just as God intended.

Hebrews 4:15 says, "For we do not have a high priest who is unable to sympathize with our weaknesses, but one who in every respect has been tempted as we are, yet without sin." It is mind-boggling that God, the Creator and Controller of time, can understand and even sympathize with our relationship to time. Christ, for His Father's glory, stepped into time, becoming subject to its limits and changed by its passing (like being a baby, maturing in body and mind for starters!) in order that He could reconcile His beloved and chosen children to Himself.

Part of Christ's humanity, and part of how He can intercede for us, is He experienced all the positive and negative effects time has on the human body and mind. Galatians 4:4–6 says, "But when the fullness of time had come, God sent forth his Son, born of woman, born under the law, to redeem those who were under the law, so that we might receive adoption as sons." We can see in this passage God uses time for His purposes in redemption. Christ stepped into earthly time so He could save us from death.

Death is not limited to an event that occurs at the end of life. Scripture tells us we are spiritually dead even while we are physically living. Ephesians 2:1 says, "And you were dead in the trespasses and sins." We are born into the world dead in our sin, but in God's timing—a process all in His hands and His will, as well as in His time—He changes us, gives us new birth, and makes us alive in Christ. If we are chosen in Him, God truly causes us to go from spiritual death to spiritual life within and during the time we are on this earth. The time during which we are spiritually dead, and before we, as Christians, are born again, is a time in our perspective we did not "serve the Lord" and we may think of as wasted time. But, it is not wasted time in God's plan and timing. Thus, time we may think was taken from us or we were deprived of was also His sovereignly assigned time.

Salvation, more specifically sanctification, takes a lifetime. The fact salvation is both once in time and a continual process during our time on this earth is fundamental to the understanding of our Christian lives as spiritual newborns (often termed "reborn"), adopted sons and daughters of God. God utilizes time to make His chosen children more and more like Himself.

It is marvelous and profound that God takes us from spiritual death to spiritual life.

So, as Christians, it is marvelous and profound that God takes us from spiritual death to spiritual life. But, what does this mean for our physical death? With the effects of the fall and sin, there is little we can do to stop the aging process associated with our time on this earth, no matter what the commercials promise. As Gini's brain tumor came back and the radiation damage to her frontal brain continued to progress, it made it difficult for her to find and speak words, focus, swallow, and take steps. Her outward decay was obvious, but we know from 2 Corinthians 4, the inner woman was "being renewed day by day" (v. 16). We saw that His glorious riches indeed strengthened her with power in her inner being. Christ dwelt in her through faith, allowing her to rest and trust in Him.

Christ is the "I AM" who meets our every need. I received an Easter card from one of my daughters with the handwritten note "Happy Resurrection Day!" and a quote from Charles Spurgeon: "I have a great need for Christ, I have a great Christ for my need."

We can see throughout the Bible that Christ is a healer both physically and spiritually. However, Jesus does not guarantee us physical health and fitness; instead, He promises us eternal life with our heavenly Father. He is who we cling to as death nears and illness slowly or quickly ravages our bodies. I was able to hold Gini's hand until the moment of death, but only Jesus held her hand as she stepped through death into eternity. Her ready smile allowed me to know, despite the physical dying process taking her time away, God was filling her with the measure of all His fullness in His own timing. And, just as her spiritual birth occurred, transferring her from death to life, so her physical death has resulted in eternal life. Her death only lasted for an instant; it truly was only a shadow, as the soul that gave her body life was immediately in the presence of the Lord.

As Gini awaited her physical death, we both rested in the knowledge of God's sovereignty over death and time. Our souls are created for eternity, outside the bounds of earthly time, and where, as a new creation in Christ Jesus (2 Corinthians 5:17), we will dwell with our new resurrected bodies.

Our yearning for eternity is why we struggle with, or often choose to ignore, the concept of our limited time on earth and our ultimate death. When these two ideas of a time limit and certain death wreak havoc on our bodies and minds, let us instead hold fast to the fact our longings for eternity will one day be fulfilled, and then we will truly know and understand what it is to be alive!

O soul, are you weary and troubled?
No light in the darkness you see?
There's light for a look at the Savior,
And life more abundant and free!

Turn your eyes upon Jesus,
Look full in His wonderful face,
And the things of earth will grow
    strangely dim,
In the light of His glory and grace.

Through death into life everlasting
He passed, and we follow Him there;
O'er us sin no more hath dominion—
For more than conqu'rors we are!

His Word shall not fail you—He
    promised;
Believe Him, and all will be well:
Then go to a world that is dying,
His perfect salvation to tell!
    — Helen Lemmel
    "Turn Your Eyes upon Jesus"

"For we know that if the earthly tent
we live in is destroyed, we have a building
from God, an eternal house in heaven,
not built by human hands. Meanwhile
we groan, longing to be clothed instead
with our heavenly dwelling, because
when we are clothed, we will not be found
naked. For while we are in this tent, we
groan and are burdened, because we do
not wish to be unclothed but to be clothed
instead with our heavenly dwelling, so
that what is mortal may be swallowed up
by life. Now the one who has fashioned
us for this very purpose is God, who has
given us the Spirit as a deposit, guarantee-
ing what is to come." (2 Corinthians 5:1–5
NIV)

"As the slide show of my life with my Mom often plays in my head, the one frame that is the most vivid is of her on her knees on the kitchen floor, huddled over the floor heating vent, with her face in her Bible. She was always my 'go-to' whenever there was something I didn't understand in the Bible. Over the past four years, I have probably missed this part of our relationship the most. But I also get a little chuckle because if I was able to communicate with her about the sadness I feel over this, I know she really wouldn't be very sympathetic and most likely would quote her oft-repeated phrase: 'I'm just one beggar showing another beggar where to find bread!' She was so faithful to show me, and I'm pretty confident that she was also faithful to show many of you in this room today, where to find that bread! So, I really think that was one of the main reasons for her unexplainable joy and peace during her illness these last four years. She was confident that she had led the way down the path of truth and those who come behind her are following in her footsteps."

— Heather Baillie Fletcher
    MA Elementary Education, Flint, Texas
    (excerpt from funeral tribute for her mother,
    Gini Baillie)

"For by grace you have been saved through faith.
And this is not your own doing; it is the gift of God,
not a result of works, so that no one may boast.
For we are His workmanship, created in Christ Jesus
for good works, which God prepared beforehand,
that we should walk in them."

— EPHESIANS 2:8–10

CHAPTER 4

The Purpose of the Gift of Time

"I wish it need not have happened
in my time," said Frodo.
"So do I," said Gandalf,
"and so do all who live to see such times.
But that is not for them to decide.
All we have to decide is what to do
with the time that is given us."[4]

— J. R. R. TOLKIEN,
THE FELLOWSHIP OF THE RING

Understanding time is a gift from God totally changes how we use and think about the time allotted us while on this earth. If we truly believe time belongs to God, then it should make it difficult for us to waste time or use it for our own selfish gain. God gives us time for His purposes and glory.

Ephesians 5:15–16 says, "Look carefully then how you walk, not as unwise but as wise, making

the best use of the time, because the days are evil."
Because God gives us time, we, as believers, should
be good stewards of time and must be deliberate
about its usage. In other words, we should have

> We should have a sense of responsibility in managing our time and intentionally considering how and whether it is honoring the Lord.

a sense of responsibility in
managing our time and in-
tentionally considering how
and whether it is honoring
the Lord.

We have often heard
someone speak about his or
her time with someone be-
fore they died. It may include
the phrase, "I just wish I had spent more time with
_____ , and now that is not possible."

However, because we know the Lord is the
sovereign Giver of time, then we can trust every
minute of it does have purpose. Even in the minutes that seem mundane, God's plan is still in
motion. No matter where we are or what we are
doing, the time can be used to bring fame to our
Father's name. It is not only during Bible study or
on mission trips when we can use our time to hon-
or the Lord. Colossians 3:17 says, "And whatever
you do, whether in word or deed, do everything in
the name of the Lord Jesus, giving thanks to God
the Father through Him." This means whatever we

are doing—working in what we think is a meaningless job, doing house or yard work, just eating a meal—God can be glorified in and with that time.

We understand all our day-to-day activities and work point to the Creator of those events or nonevents, pleasures or times of sadness, meaningful jobs or unemployment. When we work, no matter how trivial it may seem, we reflect the image of God who created us and who is still working all things for His glory and our good.

Let us not forget the night and the time we are asleep. Using about a third of our life sleeping may seem like a waste of time, but God in His wisdom has provided that period of time for our rest from daily activities to provide what is needed for our upcoming day. Psalm 127:2 says, "It is in vain that you rise up early and go late to rest, eating the bread of anxious toil; for He gives to His beloved sleep." A time of sleep and rest is needed to keep from being anxious in His assigned work in and through us.

Consider the time you feel you must go visit someone a month or a year after the death of his or her spouse or another loved one in their family. This is certainly time you could have done something else, considered more useful from your own selfish perspective. Or think about when you visit someone in a nursing home who has Alzheimer's and does not even know who you are. Are these encounters a waste of time?

God does not redeem only the time that seems mundane and ordinary but even the time we perceive as tragic (see how God promises to redeem the time the locusts have eaten in Joel 2:25, earlier quoted in chap. 2). Genesis 50:20 says, "As for you, you meant evil against me, but God meant it for good, to bring it about that many people should be kept alive, as they are today." In the story from which this verse comes, we know, even in the midst of the conflict, God used each struggle and conflict in Joseph's life to protect His children. This is because we know the ending.

However, in the midst of our own tragedy, our own uncertainty and tears sometimes muddle our vision in such a way it can be difficult to see how God could even begin to use it for His glory, let alone our good. We cannot fathom any different ending as it seems the end has already come.

In these times, it is more important we trust, despite our cloudy vision, that God's promises are true. Romans 8:28–29 promises, "We know that for those who love God, all things work together for good, for those who are called according to His purpose. For those whom He foreknew He also predestined to be conformed to the image of His Son, in order that He might be the firstborn among many brothers."

Sometimes, when we have come through a difficulty, we can clearly see how the Lord used that time to bring about good. At other times the only thing we can know is, somehow, He used time and circumstances to make us more like His Son, who was the true man of sorrows. Is it possible we, like Paul, can rejoice in times of suffering because those times make us more like our Savior? We can, but only when we acknowledge the time given to us is time we might walk in the good plan He works in and through us. Over time, God is redeeming our thoughts so the times once perceived as tragic or mundane can be seen for what they truly are: gifts from a loving Father.

Is it possible we, like Paul, can rejoice in times of suffering because those times make us more like our Savior?

One day at the oncologist's office, I signed Gini in, and as we waited for the call to go back to the chemotherapy room, I took the time to observe the evidences of impending death all around us. Some patients, strikingly thin or completely bald, were in obvious pain or distress. Gini, at the time, wore a wig to cover her bald, scarred, and radiation-damaged head, but she still wore a smile.

That day, she was also on a drug called Avastin that was causing an increase of protein in her urine and elevated blood pressure. We knew the drug would have to be discontinued, and after the cessation of this drug, Gini's tumor would return. When that occurred, we would not have it removed again because of its location and the additional damage it would do to her brain, resulting in further loss of mental functions. We were

Understanding some of our journey steps on this earth and how time is a gift requires a certain amount of humility.

both at peace with this because we knew the Lord appointed the days of our lives by exact number before the foundation of the world. Taking the tumor out again would also accelerate her memory loss and affect her mood and inhibitions, as the surgeons would have to remove normal brain tissue as well.

So we sat there, not wasting time but using it in its appointed way. We prayed the Lord would bless us with many new days, not only that we could be blessed with another day of life but that we might be a blessing to others. While in the waiting room, someone came by to say hello and comment on Gini's beautiful smile. I still continue to marvel how the Lord gave her such a peaceful countenance and smile that attracted people. The Lord used the time He gave us, even in the doctor's office waiting room, to work through us to minister to and bless others.

Understanding some of our journey steps on this earth and how time is a gift requires a certain amount of humility. As we live this life and go on toward death, we have a progressive knowledge that our lives have served some definite purpose. Sometimes, however, it seems just as this new life in Christ has sprouted, takes root, grows and matures in us, we also begin to lose our vitality, much like green summer leaves die and become autumn leaves. While our time is a purposeful and useful gift from God, it is also only a pixel in the whole picture of the history of His universe.

When we die, people will remember us for a period of time, just like the once green but now colored leaves on the ground can still be identified. Let me expound on this concept a bit.

Unless we have a penchant for genealogy, most of us only know a few details of the what, why, or even the when of our grandparents and almost nothing—often not even the names—of our great-grandparents. We have seen how death can take away our time on earth, but at the same time, while some of our time on this earth is remembered, like the rotting leaves, the specifics of that time will soon be forgotten.

But we also know, through our death (like the decayed leaves), the Lord has a purpose for each of us to provide the next generation with spiritual nourishment, even though in the grand scheme of things it is only a blip on the radar screen of life. A dead autumn leaf on the ground can still be specifically identified as to its type of tree. Although its identity fades and then disappears with time and decay, it is still important to nourish the ground and thus the next generation of leaves.

However, just because our lives, and even our deaths, will likely not be remembered by future generations, it does not take away the responsibility we have to spend our given time for Kingdom work. God is in charge of how we will nourish the coming generations. As death grows closer, we increasingly know how precious time is. Spending time with others, especially our families and fellow believers, encouraging them with the truth of the gospel, will make the little time we have on the earth count eternally.

In Matthew 28, Jesus instructs His disciples on how to use their remaining time on earth: "Go therefore and make disciples of all nations, baptizing them in the name of the Father and of the Son and of the Holy Spirit, teaching them to observe all that I have commanded you. And behold, I am with you always, to the end of the age" (vv. 19–20). By instilling in others the truth of the gospel, no matter whether it is in the workplace, at the local church, or even the doctor's office waiting room (you could add countless other opportunities), we are utilizing our precious gift of time.

> By instilling in others the truth of the gospel, . . . we are utilizing our precious gift of time.

Read how God's gift of time is presented in 1 Peter 1:3–12:

Blessed be the God and Father of our Lord Jesus Christ! According to His great mercy, He has caused us to be born again to a living hope through the resurrection of Jesus Christ from the dead, to an inheritance that is imperishable, undefiled, and unfading, kept in heaven for you, who by

God's power are being guarded through
faith for a salvation ready to be revealed
in the last *time*. In this you rejoice, though
now for a *little while*, if necessary, you
have been grieved by various trials, so
that the tested genuineness of your faith—
more precious than gold that perishes
though it is tested by fire—may be found
to result in praise and glory and honor at
the revelation of Jesus Christ. Though you
have not seen Him, you love him. Though
you do not now see Him, you believe in
Him and rejoice with joy that is inexpress-
ible and filled with glory, obtaining the
outcome of your faith, the salvation of
your souls.

Concerning this salvation, the proph-
ets who prophesied about the grace that
was to be yours searched and inquired
carefully, inquiring what person or *time*
the Spirit of Christ in them was indicat-
ing when he predicted the sufferings of
Christ and the subsequent glories. It was
revealed to them that they were serving
not themselves but you, in the things that
have now been announced to you through

those who preached the good news to
you by the Holy Spirit sent from heaven,
things into which angels long to look.
(emphasis mine, noting specific reference
to the small amount of time we have on
this earth)

Life, your gift from God.
Living, your purpose,
    responsibly fulfilling the time
    He gives you in this world.
Death, your legacy,
    leaving behind a spiritual heritage
    that counts eternally.
        — *GENE BAILLIE*

"Jesus said to her,
'I am the resurrection and the life.
Whoever believes in me, though he die,
yet shall he live, and everyone who lives
and believes in me shall never die.
Do you believe this?'"

— *JOHN 11:25–26*

CHAPTER 5

If Only You Had Been Here on Time

"Our Lord has written the promise of resurrection,
not in books alone, but in every leaf in springtime."
— UNKNOWN AUTHOR

In John 11, we are told one day Jesus received a message his good friend Lazarus was ill. His sisters Mary and Martha wanted Jesus to come to Bethany to heal Lazarus before he died. Instead of quickly rushing to His dying friend's side, Jesus stayed where He was for another two days. By the time Jesus finally arrived in Bethany, Lazarus had already been in the grave for four days. When the sisters got word Jesus was a short distance away, Martha went out to meet Him and said, "Lord, if You had been here, my brother would not have died" (v. 21). There seems to be a feeling that if only Jesus had come sooner, left immediately, or made better time on the trip, He could have healed Lazarus and saved him from death. Many of us share Martha's sentiment. We often think, *Lord, if only You had been here on time . . . .*

When Jesus spoke with the weeping sisters and other friends, Scripture tells us He was so deeply moved and troubled He wept also. Jesus — who was present at the creation of time as well as the entering of death into the world, the sovereign Ruler of both of those things, the One who at the touch of His hand can heal all diseases — wept. Although Jesus knew Lazarus would soon be alive once more, He deeply felt the implications death has on our lives. He is truly our sympathizer and great High Priest.

For those who have faith in Jesus, death is not the end. Knowing this, however, does not mean it cannot break our hearts. Death is the result of the world's brokenness, and this fact should move us to tears, even if we know our loved ones will be alive once again.

Once at Lazarus's tomb, Jesus commanded the stone be rolled away. The sisters protested because the rancid smell would only add to their troubles. After assuring them they would see the glory of God displayed, Jesus "cried out with a loud voice, 'Lazarus, come out'" (v. 43). Lazarus, still wrapped in the grave linens, appeared as if he had been asleep.

Jesus used Lazarus's death as a way to bring glory to His Father, to show His power over death, and even to demonstrate—though time allowed Lazarus to die—time does not limit God. Jesus, after Martha suggested His timing was late, told her, "I

Jesus is truly our sympathizer and great High Priest.

am the resurrection and the life. Whoever believes in me, though he die, yet shall he live, and everyone who lives and believes in me shall never die. Do you believe this?" This question still resounds today. Do you believe God is truly sovereign over both time and death?

Lazarus's death took time from the disciples and his sisters. Moreover, those four days in the grave took time from Lazarus's earthly life. It also took time away from Jesus' ministry, but it was critical and necessary time in God's economy of the seemingly short time allowed for Jesus to be on the earth. He could have done other things with His time here, but the things He did were in the perfect plan of God—as is every moment of our lives on this earth.

Although in this passage we do learn of the power of Jesus to make alive what was dead, be careful again not to fall into a false thinking trap. To repeat an important point: Death does not have the power to take life any more than its failure to be able to steal time! Death appears to take time in both senses I have written about, but death has been swallowed up in the victory of our risen Lord, death has lost its sting, death has no power, death has no control, death is but a shadow as we pass from life to life!

> We can confidently arise each morning realizing even our night's rest was not a waste of time.

If you have not heard "In His Time," a song written by Diane Ball, it will be well worth your time to find and read the lyrics. They confirm the sovereign direction of the Lord every moment of each day, in our every thought, word, and deed — and each moment is all in His perfect timing and within His created time. We see His beautiful creation all around us, He teaches us in a myriad of ways, and He brings Himself into our lives within and through His perfectly timed plan.

Because we are living in His granted time period on this earth and because He has a perfect plan for our lives, then we can confidently arise each morning realizing even our night's rest was not a waste of time. Rather, rest too is but a part of His blessing, renewing our earthly bodies in order to carry out the day's every thought, word, and deed—also to be a blessing to everyone around us. We can truly be a blessing because He has blessed us with life and breath and everything needed to carry out His purposes in His created time.

"What at first seems to be the end,
is instead just the beginning!"
— *GENE BAILLIE*

"For if we have been united with Him in a death like His, we shall certainly be united with Him in a resurrection like His. We know that our old self was crucified with Him in order that the body of sin might be brought to nothing, so that we would no longer be enslaved to sin. For one who has died has been set free from sin. Now if we have died with Christ, we believe that we will also live with Him. We know that Christ, being raised from the dead, will never die again; death no longer has dominion over Him. For the death He died He died to sin, once for all, but the life He lives He lives to God. So you also must consider yourselves dead to sin and alive to God in Christ Jesus. Let not sin therefore reign in your mortal body, to make you obey its passions. Do not present your members to sin as instruments for unrighteousness, but present yourselves to God as those who have been brought from death to life, and your members to God as instruments for righteousness. For sin will have no dominion over you, since you are not under law but under grace."

— ROMANS 6:5–14

CHAPTER 6

Time for Stripping

"As Christian believers, may we see the need
to be stripped of all that prevents and binds us
from seeing, feeling, and walking. Recognize the Lord
is the Light for our path, holding our hand
and directing each step we take."

— GENE BAILLIE

In the previous chapter, we quickly passed over the command Jesus made to have the grave clothes of Lazarus unbound or removed. In one version, the word is translated as "strip." The grave clothes were put on over spices and perfumes used to prevent some of the odors of death and decay. I find it interesting there is specific mention his hands, feet, and head were bound.

As he was brought forth, the removal of the grave clothes is symbolic of again feeling, walking, and seeing. During our lifetimes, we are clothed in dirty rags, and at death that "clothing" must be stripped away so we can be clothed in the righteousness of Christ, ours since the moment of our salvation. At this point, I would like to quote excerpts of chapter 8 of my book titled *Nothing Matters* (2015, www.ReadNothingMatters.com*)*, as it pertains to the undressing or stripping process of our soul of everything worldly as we end our time on earth.

> The "worst" ending for Christians is to immediately be in the presence of the Lord when we die, resurrected and more alive than we have ever been!

Gini Baillie, my wife for fifty-one and a half years, departed this world on May 21, 2015. I witnessed the departure of her soul from her body as she took her last breath. That soul will be given a new body. I was actually able to witness firsthand what our soul means to our earthly body during the season of our lifetime on earth—the miracle of God's creative powers with dust, water, and air, as described in Psalm 139:14 with these words: "I am fearfully and wonderfully made, . . . my soul knows it."

Many of us are scared of death, but if you are a Christian, there is no need or reason to be frightened. We have read and been taught the truth from the Bible that death has lost its sting because of the death and resurrection of Jesus Christ; but we are still scared, not satisfied with the answers and teaching we hear until we embrace the rest, peace, and trust in the hope offered to us. As we get older or as we go through trials, we begin to understand about death more clearly, but one of the best ways to be certain is to be beside someone when he dies. Some have pain, and all suffer in some way. But, if we know Jesus and truly rest and trust in Him, having faith provided to us (with its resultant hope), then He will not give us more than we can bear and will hold our hand throughout the journey!

The "worst" ending for Christians is to immediately be in the presence of the Lord when we die, resurrected and more alive than we have ever been! For you see, I watched my wife walk through the valley of the shadow of death without fear and with complete trust and rest in Jesus. I know, with all the more certainty, passing from this life is only a shadow! I could not clearly see as she could, but I could hold her hand until Jesus was the only one holding her hand for that last step.

I knew then, and I understand now in part, the unveiling of His glory as she was stripped of the worldly. I saw the realization and truth of 1 Corinthians 13:12—"For now we see in a mirror dimly, but then face to face. Now I know in part;

then I shall know fully, even as I have been fully known."

Nancy Guthrie edited *O Love That Will Not Let Me Go*, a collection of meditations drawn from the sermons and writings of pastors and theologians. In a chapter titled "Sickness: The Soul's Undressing," she includes some of Jeremy Taylor's comments written in the 1600s. The opening paragraph is a beautiful expression of what I witnessed at Gini's passing.

> In sickness the soul begins to dress
> herself for immortality. First, she unties
> the strings of vanity that made her up-
> per garment cleave to the world and sit
> uneasy; she puts off the light and fantastic
> summer robe of lust and wanton appetite;
> and as soon as that lascivious girdle is
> thrown away, . . . then that which called
> us formerly to serve the manliness of the
> body, and the childishness of the soul,
> keeps us waking, to divide the hours with
> . . . prayer and groans. Then the flesh
> sets uneasily and dwells in sorrow. The
> spirit feels itself at ease, freed from the
> petulant solicitations of those passions
> which in health were as busy and restless

as atoms in the sun, always dancing, and
always busy, and never sitting down, till
a sad night of grief and uneasiness draws
the veil, and lets them die alone in secret
dishonor. Next to this, the soul, by the
help of sickness, knocks off the fetters of
pride and vainer complacencies. Then she
draws the curtains, and stops the light
from coming in, and takes the pictures
down, those fantastic images of self-love
and gay remembrances of vain opinion
and popular noises.[5]

By reading and reflecting on the additional
pages of this writing on sickness, I now move on
with my observations. There continues the progressive stripping of layers of worldly philosophy,
wisdom, wit, possessions, animosities, discourse,
pride veiled as humility, anger, and so much more.

When sickness and suffering last a long time
and a deadly diagnosis is given, as in the case of
my wife, there is also the need to be stripped of the
accolades that are like hearing your eulogy spoken
before your funeral! As the stripping occurs, we
see faith demonstrating itself to be a powerful and
mighty grace at the approach of death, accompanied by a peace beyond understanding.

For in our days of health, it is easy to put trust in God for His loving care and even His provided escape from the bounds of a trial. But, as we approach the edge of our grave, then we truly see our faith and hope so much closer to the promised reality of eternal life. So, God is dressing us for heaven by the undressing and removal of all but the soul. He must have us struggle, resist the Devil, contest the weakness of nature, and against hope believe in hope, thus resigning ourselves completely to God's sovereign will. Knowing He chose us, knowing too that dying results in the fulfillment of His promises, we will be more alive than we have ever been!

A quiet grave remains, a legacy remains for a season, the pleasant lot into which we were placed is now void of our literal and bodily presence; but our soul is then at perfect peace with the Lord, enjoying and praising Him eternally.

Again, for the Christian, the labor process of the gradual stripping away of the worldly is not guaranteed to be easy or short—medicines or various treatments may or may not be required—but the actual delivery process (death) is always instantaneous. My own wife's journey was four years long after her diagnosis of the deadly brain cancer called glioblastoma. Although the journey was largely peaceful, she did have intermittent difficult steps as I held her hand. These included blood clots in her lungs, disorientation, bone marrow failure, seizures, a broken hip, and pneumonia. But she was at rest and peace in her Jesus who was able to meet her every need.

Jesus also provided for Gini's loving care, which included His enabling me. Her death was a beautiful process; and although it was not fun, sitting at her bedside in our home, holding her hand, was a time of joy and rejoicing that our Lord was finished with her work on this earth. Everything was for her good and the good of all of those who came in contact with her—and was for His glory. All believers are sent to and through death to secure eternal life.

> Everything was for Gini's good and the good of all of those who came in contact with her—and was for His glory.

Not so for the unbeliever, however. I can only imagine what happens to his soul, but I am certain it is in a place of no joy, no hope, and unending sorrow and torment. I also know without love for and faith in the Lord that no hope exists. For the unbeliever dying without a saving knowledge of Jesus Christ, the new residence for eternity will be a place called hell. Our understanding is sometimes most enhanced when we are presented with the conditions of the polar opposite. Therefore, if you are an unbeliever reading this, I pray your eyes will be opened and your ears hear the truth of the descriptions of hell in the Bible, that place of unending torment and gnashing of teeth, the place (described in Luke 16:19–31) where a rich man in torment in hell requests of another man named Lazarus to provide only the water on the tip of a finger be put on his tongue!

The last verses of Isaiah describe the final judgment and the time coming when each of us will be in only one of two places forever. Read Isaiah 66:15–24 but especially verse 24: "And they shall go out and look on the dead bodies of the men who have rebelled against me. For their worm shall not die, their fire shall not be quenched, and they shall be an abhorrence to all flesh."

Finally, take note of Revelation 14:9–11:

> And another angel, a third, followed them, saying with a loud voice, "If any-one worships the beast and its image and receives a mark on his forehead or on his hand, he also will drink the wine of God's wrath, poured full strength into the cup of his anger, and he will be tormented with fire and sulfur in the presence of the holy

angels and in the presence of the Lamb.
And the smoke of their torment goes up
forever and ever, and they have no rest,
day or night, these worshipers of the beast
and its image, and whoever receives the
mark of its name."

And then, read the next two verses, 12 and
13, to see the contrast written to believers (called
saints).

We humans also love our sin, and we believers know the wages of sin is death. If we remain
wrapped up in our own small package, without
the God-given gift of saving faith, we will not gain
His reward. Like Lazarus we must have our death
clothes stripped away. Faith comes as a free gift,
but changes are demanded. We cannot stay in our
sinful environment; instead, we must desire to
progress on our journey's path toward Christ and
His work for us to do. Then the wages received is a
guaranteed eternal life! Walk in the footsteps of the
faith the Lord gives and live.

Each morning I read some of the Bible to Gini,
and at night, family members said the Twenty-
third Psalm with Gini before singing the *Blessing*
song by Twila Paris about grace and peace. What
peace I observed growing within Gini as we read

not only this psalm but from her extensive list of memorized passages. And the same was true for me. In Psalm 23, one verse became increasingly important to me as I experienced the changes in both

As we both became older, we began to realize more clearly the things of earth were not the most important anymore.

my wife and myself. Verse 3 says, "He restores my soul. He leads me in paths of righteousness." As I reflect, I become more and more aware of how God truly restores our souls. A process of stripping of the worldly occurred in Gini. The things of earth became progressively more dim and unimportant. She closed her eyes often but was always listening. The best balm for the soul is words of comfort!

I want to now tell you this same stripping was and is occurring in me, just in an earlier stage. I know we were going through this process together all our married years. As we both became older, we began to realize more clearly the things of earth were not the most important anymore; however, we were still holding the worldly quite tightly.

Now, within myself, I can see how the Lord has begun to strip away the layers of my own worldly life. He is stripping; and as my body, too, will take its last breath, my soul also will be absent from the body, restored to my Creator. The body is useful to the Lord while He has us on this earth; He then returns the empty shell to the earth. For the Christian, He takes our soul to be with Him in eternity. At that moment, He not only perfects and completes us but promises to give our soul a new body.

He is leading me in paths of righteousness. He is restoring my soul as He does with all His children, preparing me for departing this world. I also see the beginnings of the fading of any fear of death and the rising peace, trust, and rest within my very being. Gini was a little ahead of me on this journey, and I perceive the end of my journey is only a little way up the path, just beyond the next bend.

As you finish this chapter, dear reader, it is my prayer each day you also progressively and more clearly see the Lord's direction and purpose—in your life, for your time, and through your death. May you loose your grip on the worldly, knowing you too will be stripped of all but your soul before death.

"Truly, truly, I say to you,
unless a grain of wheat falls into the earth and dies,
it remains alone; but if it dies, it bears much fruit.
Whoever loves his life loses it, and whoever hates
his life in this world will keep it for eternal life.
If anyone serves me, he must follow me;
and where I am, there will my servant be also.
If anyone serves me, the Father will honor him."

— *JOHN 12:24–26*

CHAPTER 7

Comments and Summary

*"Why you dying, Mama?" Forrest asked.
"My time, it's just my time. . . .
Death is just a part of life. . . . You have to do the best
with what God gave you," Mama answered. . . .
"Mama always said, dying was a part of life.
I sure wish it wasn't."*[6]

— FORREST GUMP

Each day brings us one day closer to death, which is encroaching on our earthly time. Seeing our bodies dying a little each day makes us realize with increasing intensity we are approaching the end. We know the truth of so many Scriptures concerning death and our coming eternal life. But can we be at peace with our upcoming death, trusting and resting in our loving and gracious Lord's plan? I consider my wife an example of a person able to die to self as she saw and reaped the fruit of her submission to the Lord.

Gini also had a storehouse of countless memorized verses and whole books of Scripture that included every verse I have used in this book. These verses and memorized Christian music lyrics were thankfully in a different part of her brain from the damaged area. Before her tumor was discovered and also before she lost her ability to speak, she said many times that memory verses are not "if you need them but when."

After we become Christians and are transferred from spiritual death to spiritual life, we are given the admonition to die to self each day as we serve the Lord. We are to seek His will and direction and forego our own. Similarly, as each day we "die" a little more physically, the spiritual practice we have learned and lived will be used by the Lord to not only prepare us but also to provide us rest and trust in Him as we face death in whatever form and in whatever timing. We will have peace that transcends our understanding. We know the Lord is holding our hand and will do so for that last step of our earthly journey. We truly can know, in less than an instant, we will pass through and from that shadow of death to eternal life.

Prolonging life is really prolonging death, but we are not to take things into our own hands. Many times Gini seemed to be confused, but she still wanted and appreciated my comforting hand holding hers. And even when confused, she could express herself in drawings and scribbled words that conveyed she was still with us. This was not a time to make any rash decisions.

We truly can know, in less than an instant, we will pass through and from that shadow of death to eternal life.

When someone is unresponsive, and when you are sure there is no hope of return except by a miracle of the Lord, that is the time you turn them over to Him, the Sovereign over time. You need not prolong death only to have a breathing but nearly lifeless person in the room with you. However, each day God allows healing and medicine to prolong life is a day of death prolonged.

Just as I wrote in the previous chapter about observing from afar the stripping of the soul of my beloved wife, I was able to discern and be at peace as Gini's death approached. I simply held her hand, prayed with her, sang to her, and assured her Jesus was taking her home. I did not panic at those last gasps for air, and I did not call 911. As He did for us, the Lord will provide you His direction in this time of need, whether peaceful or quite difficult, even with extreme anguish.

Another important issue is being prepared in advance so you can finish well. By this I mean not only that you know Jesus as your Savior, Lord, and very Treasure (free gift of God), and not only that you have biblical knowledge applied to your life and the way you live, but you have everything in order and prepared for leaving this earth. And what you have not done, or not finished as you desired, you simply turn over to the Lord. We must pray and ask the Lord to help us not be angry, not be distressed by unfinished repair of relationships, not to be negative or to use wrong words, not to fear death. The best way I understand this can be accomplished is to use the time you have right now in the days the Lord has you on this earth in the proper way. What is the proper way? To follow and serve the Lord in every thought, word, and deed.

Let me tell you best by my own observations, my own heart, and my own desire. I have spent time in this book discussing the process and reality of death, especially the death of my wife, the first person I ever watched die. You might say, "Gene, you were a doctor!" I would reply I examined the living prior to death and pronounced them dead after death occurred, but I had not held the hand of the dying until my wife. So, what now follows is my reflection on, dealing with, and considering my own death, as well as use of my own time.

The entire experience of death has forced me to really think about also wanting to finish well. I have sought to lead a godly life, study God's Word to be approved, share with others, and apply His truth to every facet of my life. Planning in advance for how to deal with any sin or temptation, for example sexual temptation, has allowed me to "keep on walking," not to stand, not to sit, and not to be involved in sinful desires (see Psalm 1:1). In all things, it is better to "prevent" than to "patch"! Do not stop, stand, or sit in a sinful situation, one you know can lead to a specific sin.

I have sought to have a solid and biblical family and use biblical principles to guide all other relationships. I do not have any broken relationships in my family, my foster family, or with others on this earth to the best of my knowledge and ability, and with God's help. Even the unbelievers know I love and respect them, will give them godly counsel, and will not beat around the bush!

I seek to live within my means—which helps immensely with greed, jealousy, or temptation to take what is not mine—and thus resulting contentment. At the other extreme, anything I have is provided by God, loaned for my proper use. I have to hold my gifts and possessions with open hands, not with a greedy grip. I have never been one to drink much and never to excess, so that's really not an issue, but I have had to counsel many who face this temptation because of depression, mental instability, seeming inability and failure, or feelings of poor self-worth.

But, I have had to deal with another of the underlying causes that often results in sinful behavior, of wanting to control everything. The Lord had me deal with this issue of control in 1978, but I still battle almost daily. My chief help is the Lord, realizing He is in control of absolutely every detail of my life.

> "In his heart or mind, man makes his plans, but the Lord determines, guides, and directs each step."
> — PROVERBS 16:9

My life verse is Proverbs 16:9 with my translation of the Hebrew words: "In his heart or mind, man makes his plans, but the Lord determines, guides, and directs each step." So, the answer to the problem of control in my life is to be submissive to the Lord, His Word, and to those He has placed in authority over me. Jesus as "I AM in control" is plainly and simply what the Lord has taught me.

Lastly, I need to constantly preach truth from God's Word to my heart so I will make those plans according to His will and not mine. I have read through the Bible now for the thirtieth year, but the application to my life is the key. I must be ready at all times to counsel myself and others regarding the hope that is within me (see 1 Peter 3:15). Accountability with other Christians is also key. Head knowledge alone is worthless.

How then shall I live for the remaining days, hours, and minutes the Lord has me on this earth? By knowing and truly understanding I have a clean heart, a new and clean record, and a new life because of God's plan, the sacrifice of Jesus Christ, and the work of the Holy Spirit as the actual change agent in me as a chosen and adopted son (see chap. 9 of this book). But, I am still prone to sin all my remaining days, so I must hide God's Word in my heart daily so I will not sin against Him (see Psalm 119:9, 11).

And, in regard to sin, I must not glibly say I am a sinner and ask the Lord to help me not be sinful. Instead, I must name particular sins to Him and ask for His help to combat my sinful ways. One way is to speak specific Scripture back to myself. One passage is Galatians 5:19–21, where we see sins in categories that must be dealt with. The first sins listed are those against the body and specifically sexual in nature. I am thankful I do not have any problem with pornography. I have not committed adultery, but the lustful thoughts are still there, and a sin I must deal with (see Matthew 5:27–28). Galatians 5:20 then goes on to the next category of sin I and all of us must deal with, that of idolatry or religious sins, putting anything in the place of God. This is followed by sins of mind, attitude, and behavior.

Lastly, in verse 21, we see the sins of appetite and indulgence. If you also go to Ephesians 5:3–6, you will see coveting added to the specific sin list. There are many other sins, such as cursing and pride. In fact, the Bible has hundreds of sins listed. Returning to Galatians, the fruit of the Spirit mentioned in 5:22–23 consists of nine listed fruit items. These are the end result or goal of the process of acknowledging sin, not the beginning!

Therefore my cup must be emptied of myself. I must pray for His Spirit to fill me daily, not so my cup is half full or half empty but, instead, is fully filled with the Lord's Spirit; so when I am "bumped" or asked to give counsel in my daily walk, what spills out is fully the Lord seen and heard through me. I am to trust and obey, understanding there truly is no other path—He is the way, the truth, and the life (see John 14:6). I am to trust in the Lord with all my heart and not lean on my own understanding, so that in all my ways I will always acknowledge His plan, will, and direction, knowing He will make my paths straight as He directs my every step (see Proverbs 3:5–6).

And Philippians 4:4–9 counsels me to rid myself of anxiety by rejoicing in the Lord, knowing, as I say "I am anxious," He promises "I AM your peace," providing a peace beyond all understanding that will guard my

I must pray for His Spirit to fill me daily, not so my cup is half full or half empty but, instead, is fully filled with the Lord's Spirit.

heart and mind as I live in the Spirit and walk in the Spirit. My life is to bring God glory as He works in me for my good. And, then my prayer is for others to follow my example as they see only Jesus in me. For me, this is *the* way—to wake up each morning, seeking Him in Word, prayer, and quietness, knowing I can trust and rest completely in His perfect plan, care, and comfort for all that will happen that day and each day.

He is the great "I AM," who will meet, answer, and provide for my every need (not want), working in me to accomplish His will for today and each of my days (see Romans 12, the entire chapter).

As you now finish this short book, I hope you clearly saw the many aspects of how death takes time, including the intended play on words. And how death is a process and truly has no ability to take time. Most of the following review points are also seen in the account of Lazarus in the John 11 passage.

1. You know how death takes time in the manner it deprived me of time with my uncle.
2. That same death took (deprived his) time he could have spent on this earth.
3. As my wife took longer to die than statistics indicated, death takes time, giving us time we did not expect.
4. As death approaches, whether quickly or gradually with age or disease, it takes more time to think, do, and communicate.
5. Funerals are an example of the process of death; they take up time we could have used in some other productive way, and sometimes we have a feeling our time is being wasted.
6. Death takes earthly time. Daily and at the moment of death, our earthly time is taken away. After death, we are *no longer* in the realm of earthly time.
7. Each day, the process of our upcoming death takes time in two ways. First, our death is one day closer. Second, our death has been delayed or prolonged by one day.
8. We see a day passed is time forever taken

away, as we are one day closer to death. Each day contains that portion of our earthly time taken away until we die. We cannot redeem it, but the Lord promises to do so. When I turned forty, I received a T-shirt with Roman numerals on the back. I finally figured out the number, but then I could not figure out what that number signified, even with the help of my wife who usually caught on quickly to such surprise gifts. When I called the friend who sent the shirt, he said he would tell me "in a few *days*," which of course caused me to use more precious time I thought I could have been doing something else. The number was 14,610, the number of days I lived those forty years including the ten extra for leap years!

9. God created time. God is in charge of the number of days, hours, minutes, and seconds we are alive on this earth, and we are not to waste any of the time—but we do. We are here for His purposes. It "*takes* a lifetime" for His sanctification process to be exactly what He has planned. That lifetime is the length God determines, and the phrase is an interesting play on words because death, as well, "*takes* a lifetime"!

10. Time is both exact and relative. Time as we get older is relative but, at the same time, still

has its preciseness and exactness. We can define time with precision as it is ongoing and consistent. Days have twenty-four hours with a rising and setting sun. The days become months and years with moon and season cycles. However, at the *same time,* as we get older, we perceive the relative shortness of a span of time compared to our perception of that *same time* as a youth.

11. Death takes time to visit with, time of, and time from others in your life. It takes time to sit with, to serve, and to do work the dying person would have performed in former days. It takes time you could have spent with them in a totally different way.

12. Death takes time away from other things of life. Watching someone else die (quickly or slowly) takes time away from other aspects of life, and watching ourselves die takes time. On the positive side, the certainty of death often gives us time to get our affairs in order. Both the person dying and others can address not only worldly goods but also relationships. The appendix lists some of the items that take time to arrange before we die, such as a will and inventory of assets and writing down our directives or wishes.

13. After we die, our death continues to take the time of others. Immediately is all the time associated with the funeral, arrangements, and visitation. Then, for weeks and months afterward, there is the time spent for probate of the will, making decisions, changing documents and titles, and the like. Much of the earthly evidence of our existence must be removed. More time is spent as the heirs attempt to determine the specifics of any written will and the mental or intended "will" and wishes of the now-deceased relative.

14. Death takes away time of remembering. After our death, we will only be remembered for a time and then that time of remembering will also be taken away, hopefully replaced by a legacy of God-glorifying influence in following generations (I used the leaf example in chap. 4 and on the cover). God's eternity truly conquers and "takes out" the enemy. Eternal life wins! Death is conquered. It is only a shadow and only an instant. As death has indeed taken our earthly time away, we are ushered into an eternity that replaces the time! Death has lost its sting; we are in the presence of the Lord and more alive than we can now even imagine.

How do you spend your time? There are a multitude of answers. You have time for work, family, leisure, people, sports, hobbies, reading, Facebook, e-mails, tweets, Instagram, Snapchat, texts, conversations, computer games, movies, TV, and so many more things you desire to do. Other times you feel guilty you have wasted some of your precious time you will never get back. Or you have not studied to be approved by God because you have not studied the Bible or memorized passages or prayed as you should. That is your perspective. But God is weaving every moment of your days and time on this earth for your good and His glory, despite what you might think was any "lost" time. However, I do not mean to say that you should not be intentional with time spent with your Lord.

Even though you might feel time has been cut short or wasted, or life events have interfered in some way, and even though you might feel your days lived have been prolonged or shortened, still you have a sovereign God who redeems all your days according to His will and perfect plan. This is truth for everyone and every relationship. He determined the days for you before there was even one.

What you think might be too short or too long a time is actually the perfect timing redeemed by the Lord.

Here is a biblical perspective from Romans 8:6–11:

For to set the mind on the flesh is death, but to set the mind on the Spirit is life and peace. For the mind that is set on the flesh is hostile to God, for it does not submit to God's law; indeed, it cannot. Those who are in the flesh cannot please God. You, however, are not in the flesh but in the Spirit, if in fact the Spirit of God dwells in you. Anyone who does not have the Spirit of Christ does not belong to Him. But if Christ is in you, although the body is dead because of sin, the Spirit is life because of righteousness. If the Spirit of Him who raised Jesus from the dead dwells in you, He who raised Christ Jesus from the dead will also give life to your mortal bodies through His Spirit who dwells in you.

You do not need a mind completely wrapped up in thinking about your fleshly body, a body that ultimately has an ending in death. Instead, you need to have your mind (every part of your being) completely occupied with the things of the

Holy Spirit, who is at work in and through you. Your life and all of your time on earth is indeed in His hands and in His plan. As death takes time in any of its multitude of ways, the result after that instant of physical death is life with your Lord for all eternity.

If then you have been raised with
Christ, seek the things that are above,
where Christ is, seated at the right hand
of God. Set your minds on things that are
above, not on things that are on earth. For
you have died, and your life is hidden
with Christ in God. When Christ who
is your life appears, then you also will
appear with Him in glory. Put to death
therefore what is earthly in you: sexual
immorality, impurity, passion, evil desire, and covetousness, which is idolatry.
On account of these the wrath of God is
coming. In these you too once walked,
when you were living in them. But now
you must put them all away: anger, wrath,
malice, slander, and obscene talk from
your mouth. Do not lie to one another,
seeing that you have put off the old self

with its practices and have put on the new
self, which is being renewed in knowledge
after the image of its creator. Here there is
not Greek and Jew, circumcised and uncir-
cumcised, barbarian, Scythian, slave, free;
but Christ is all, and in all. Put on then,
as God's chosen ones, holy and beloved,
compassionate hearts, kindness, humility, meekness, and patience, bearing with
one another and, if one has a complaint
against another, forgiving each other; as
the Lord has forgiven you, so you also
must forgive. And above all these put on
love, which binds everything together
in perfect harmony. And let the peace of
Christ rule in your hearts, to which indeed
you were called in one body. And be
thankful. Let the word of Christ dwell in
you richly, teaching and admonishing one
another in all wisdom, singing psalms and
hymns and spiritual songs, with thankful-
ness in your hearts to God. And whatever
you do, in word or deed, do everything
in the name of the Lord Jesus, giving
thanks to God the Father through Him.
(Colossians 3:1–17)

"Lord, let me never,
never outlive my love to Thee."

— BERNARD OF CLAIRVAUX,
WORDS FROM "O SACRED HEAD,
NOW WOUNDED" (1153)

CHAPTER 8

Afterward: Death Continues to Take Time

"O Love, that wilt not let me go,
I rest my weary soul in Thee;
I give Thee back the life I owe."

— GEORGE MATHESON,
WORDS FROM "O LOVE THAT WILL NOT
LET ME GO" (*SACRED SONGS*, 1890)

Virginia "Gini" Baillie, the wife of my life, ended her time on this earth on May 21, 2015, four years after her diagnosis with the deadly brain cancer called glioblastoma. She could not walk, talk, or eat on her own for most of the last year of her life, so the time needed for just helping her with daily living increased manyfold. I remember taking an average of one hour to simply feed her each meal. Then her final few days of earthly time required many more people and their time to help care for her in our home.

Don't get me wrong, I would not have had it any other way. During Gini's last week, I did not leave the house while I joyfully held her hand, as promised more than fifty years earlier, in sickness till death did part us. Worldly cares and decisions accumulated, and I was not able to attend events. Some could wait and I could catch up with them later, but many of the places I might ordinarily go and attend, or appointments with people, were simply missed or eliminated from my schedule.

But, death also takes time after our death. The immediate family and I had so many extra necessary things to do with the arrangements for Gini's visitation, funeral, and burial. We had spent much time in the past making some of those decisions, but now there was the onslaught. And then there was the myriad of telephone calls and texts, forms to fill out, visits to local offices, and delivering or mailing forms and death certificates. That was followed by my three daughters and I taking time to remember special occasions attached to her possessions, along with the decisions as to what they wanted to keep to remember then and later. The layer of grandchildren and foster sons were next, with their families and children. Lots of people with lots of decisions that all took time!

Even though there was sadness, hosting (isn't that an unusual word!) her visitation was all the joy I hoped for as all fifteen of our biological family of three daughters, their husbands, and our grand-children gathered—accompanied by all four of our foster sons and their families, plus their four sib-lings and families, culminating in a grand total of thirty-nine family in the receiving line! For more than three hours, we greeted many hundreds of dear friends. It was certainly time well spent but still a lot of collective time, especially when you consider some people came from California, Mich-igan, Illinois, Texas, Tennessee, and Hawaii, as well as many other nearby states.

Then, the next day, even more came to the God-glorifying funeral, the following graveside service, and then to our home. Many from out of town spent time not only to talk with us but also spent time for travel and overnight stays.

During the following weeks and months, there was the probate and filing of Gini's will, removing her name from titles, deeds, house, stock, and bank accounts, and anything else that had been her com-plete or partial "possession" during her earthly life. Although there are recorded documents, other traces of her existence and her imprint in so many worldly ways quickly began to fade. Just another reminder our lives are not about us but about the Lord and His glory and purpose. All these things took my time as well as the time of her heirs, the accountant, the attorneys, the probate judge, and many more.

Gini and I were married for fifty-one and a half years. I witnessed the departure of Gini's soul from her body as she took her last breath, and it was confirmed when I viewed her body at the funeral home in preparation for visitation. There was still a body we could identify as hers, but it was apparent it was lifeless.

> "I have no greater joy than to hear that my children are walking in the truth."
> — 3 JOHN 1:4

I have no problem in using the word *it* because I know it was no longer a living being. I know her cancer-ridden brain was still in that body but no longer functioning.

I know we have pictures and memories "living" on. I know her legacy to all of her biological and foster children as well as her many spiritual children will live on.

But it was obvious her soul had departed her body, that part of her being I have attempted to describe to you as "nothing" or "no man" in a companion book titled *Nothing Matters*. I now know for certain "nothing" is really something absent from the body but present with the Lord. That soul will be given a new body.

I was actually able to witness firsthand what our soul means to our earthly body during the season of our lifetime on earth. I will take time to visit her grave with the inscription from 3 John 1:4, "I have no greater joy than to hear that my children are walking in the truth." More importantly, I will take time to rejoice not only in this truth but to thank the Lord for the time He allowed her to be on this earth for her good, for my and so many others' good, and for His glory. God was good to place Gini on this earth when He did, God was good to give her to me for fifty-one and a half years, and God was good to take her home to be with Him— her earthly journey and sojourn completed. Praise the Lord. (A short "extended version" video about marriage vows has Gini and my voices and can be viewed at www.ReadTheJourneyHome.com.)

Then I saw another angel flying directly overhead, with an eternal gospel to proclaim to those who dwell on earth, to every nation and tribe and language and people. And he said with a loud voice, "Fear God and give him glory, because the hour of his judgment has come, and worship him who made heaven and earth, the sea and the springs of water."

Another angel, a second, followed, saying, "Fallen, fallen is Babylon the great, she who made all nations drink the wine of the passion of her sexual immorality." And another angel, a third, followed them, saying with a loud voice, "If anyone worships the beast and its image and receives a mark on his forehead or on his hand, he also will drink the wine of God's wrath, poured full strength into the cup of his anger, and he will be tormented with fire and sulfur in the presence of the holy angels and in the presence of the Lamb. And the smoke of their torment goes up forever and ever, and they have no rest, day or night, these worshipers of the beast and its image, and whoever receives the mark of its name." Here is a call for the endurance of the saints, those who keep the commandments of God and their faith in Jesus. And I heard a voice from heaven saying,

"Write this: Blessed are the dead who die in the Lord from now on." "Blessed indeed," says the Spirit, "that they may rest from their labors, for their deeds follow them!" Then I looked, and behold, a white cloud, and seated on the cloud one like a son of man, with a golden crown on his head, and a sharp sickle in his hand. And another angel came out of the temple, calling with a loud voice to him who sat on the cloud, "Put in your sickle, and reap, for the hour to reap has come, for the harvest of the earth is fully ripe." So he who sat on the cloud swung his sickle across the earth, and the earth was reaped.

Then another angel came out of the temple in heaven, and he too had a sharp sickle. And another angel came out from the altar, the angel who has authority over the fire, and he called with a loud voice to the one who had the sharp sickle, "Put in your sickle and gather the clusters from the vine of the earth, for its grapes are ripe." So the angel swung his sickle across the earth and gathered the grape harvest of the earth and threw it into the great winepress of the wrath of God. And the winepress was trodden outside the city, and blood flowed from the winepress, as high as a horse's bridle, for 1,600 stadia.

— REVELATION 14:6–20

CHAPTER 9

Afterword: Share the Eternal Gospel Message

Allow what you have read in this short book, what others have shared with you, and what the Bible teaches to sink deep into your heart and mind. Life is a gift. Life is brief. Now that you know the Lord has set you apart, use your gifts and your remaining time wisely. Pray. Study His Word. Share the good news.

There are many suggested ways to share your changed heart with others the Lord places in your path. What follows is one that makes sense and works for me, allowing me to keep the basic principles in my head as I have opportunities to tell others about the hope that is within me. One way does not fit us all, but it is God's plan and command to have us share with others. Review this outline and see if at least parts of this "blueprint" can be used to "build you up" and be "foundational" for others. But also remember, "Unless the LORD builds the house, those who build it labor in vain" (Psalm 127:1).

First, let me state the obvious. To build a house you first have the desire to have a house and then a plan, or blueprint. Next you select a place and lay a good foundation. Finally, the more visible part of the house is built, useful for its intended purpose. I am such a house (the Bible also refers to me as a temple or tent—see 1 Corinthians 3:16–17; 2 Corinthians 5:1; 1 Peter 2:5). My house was started by God and is built on a firm foundation of His Word and prayer, and according to a perfect plan. I am useful to the Builder's purpose. I am to have an "open house" to show how I am constructed and then share the plan. Now, to share my "blueprint."

Man's Eternal Blueprint

About thirty years ago as I was struggling with the best way to share my faith and the gospel message, Gini and I audited a seminary class. One of the sessions by "Dr K" was on biblical evangelism, to help us as we seek to share the gospel message. Each of us learns and shares in different ways; this one I could comprehend easier than others. So I am sharing the basic tenets he taught from Ezekiel 36, principles I have modified into what I call "Man's Eternal Blueprint."

The following diagram is a presentation of the gospel message I keep in my mind, and after sharing, I hand out, printed on blue paper. It is based on my changes to material presented by Dr. Henry Krabbendam, professor emeritus of Biblical Studies at Covenant College, Lookout Mountain, Georgia. For more than thirty years, he shared these truths not only with seminary students and on many mission trips to Uganda but also each year as his introductory message to incoming freshman students.

The outline has numbered steps with supporting Bible references in the left margin area. I have typed out a summary of each of the numbers along with the Scripture references to help you with the flow of the outline.

1. In the beginning, God created the heavens and the earth. Apart from Him, not anything came into being. God created Adam and Eve (little boxes with letters *A* and *E*) and placed them in the Garden of Eden. Adam and Eve disobeyed God (sinned), He banished them from the garden, and they lost fellowship with God. This is symbolized by seeing they

are now separated from God on the other side of the fellowship line (Gen 1:1; John 1:3; Gen 2:13; Gen 3:23–24).

2. Because of Adam and Eve sinning, we are all born as sinners (Ps 51:5; Rom 5:12; Rom 3:23), out of fellowship with God. As sinners we have three problems:

    a. a rebellious, deceitful (bad) heart, Jer 17:9

    b. a guilty (bad) record, Rom 3:10–18; Jas 2:10; Rom 8:7–8

    c. an unholy, disobedient (bad) life, John 15:5; Eph 2:8–9

3. Since spiritual death came to all mankind through sin, we are born sinful (the letter *C* is used for us as born children). If we die separated from God, we cross over the death line where we will spend eternity in hell out of fellowship with God. This separation from God cannot be restored by anything we try to do because we are spiritually dead with a bad heart, a bad record, and a bad life.

4. It is important to note that without the intervention of God we are unable and unwilling to live a life holy and pleasing to God. Our heart is turned from and rebellious to God. Our record is one of transgressions and offenses against God. If we die in this state, we go

to a place called hell. Death only lasts for an instant, and then we spend eternity in either heaven or hell. Hell is a place of no fellowship with God, no mercy, physical misery, and spiritual misery (Rev 21:27; Dan 12:2; Rev 20:14–15; Mark 9:48–49; Luke 16:19–31; 2 Thess 1:7–9; Matt 7:23; Rev 21:8).

5. Now we consider a question that must be asked and then pray that the Lord will open eyes and ears to see and hear the gospel message in its simplicity through the work of God as Father (*F*), Jesus Christ the Son (*S*), and the Holy Spirit (*HS*). The question is, "How can we get rid of these three problems and be moved back into fellowship with God?" It is certain there is not anything we can do that will accomplish the changes needed. It is a work of God in the following ways (6-8).

6. God the Father chooses whom will be brought back to fellowship with Him, according to His perfect plan. God the Father has chosen many (*election*), but not all will see, hear, or understand His *perfect plan* for a new heart, a clean, blameless record and a holy, obedient life (Eph 1:4, 11; Rev 7:9; Ezek 36:25–27).

7. God the Son (Jesus Christ) provided for *redemption* 2,000 years ago. This redemption

is provided to the *elect* who see, hear, and understand Jesus Christ is their Lord, Savior, and Treasure. Jesus is the one who destroys our old heart on the cross, is our substitute granting a blameless record (righteousness), and is our source of holiness (Rom 6:6, 11; Isa 53:10–13; 1 Pet 1:3; John 10:14–15; 2 Cor 5:17–21; Eph 1:3; John 15:5; Phil 4:13).

8. But, neither step 6 or 7 occurs in an individual until God the Holy Spirit regenerates, guarantees, and encourages. God the Holy Spirit causes our *renewal* (regeneration) by implanting a *new heart* within us (we call this being born again) and is evidenced by repentance and faith, followed by calling on the name of Jesus for salvation (1 Pet 1:23; Luke 13:3, 5; Acts 1:8; Acts 2:38; Eph 2:8–9; Rom 10:13; Acts 2:21).

9. As truly being born again (saved), now God through His Holy Spirit seals and restores our fellowship with God through the accomplished and completed work of Jesus Christ, who we now acknowledge as our Savior, Lord, and the free gift of God (Treasure) (Rom 5:1–2; 1 Cor 6:11; Heb 7:25).

10. We are now an adopted child of God (letter C, connected to God) through the intercessory work of Christ. We also see and understand

God's perfect plan is at work in us in a process called sanctification.

11. We now see, hear, and understand the *clean,
    blameless record* of Jesus Christ is now ours and
    is guaranteed by the Holy Spirit (Eph 1:13–14).

12. We can now live a *holy, obedient life* which is
    evidenced in us by a desire to hear, read, and
    study God's Word, as well as casting off temp-
    tation, a desire to obey God's law, effective
    prayer, a desire for Christian fellowship, acting
    like the new creation we are, and bearing fruit
    (Jas 1:12–15; Rom 8:4; Ps 119:9–11; Luke 18:1–7;
    Jas 5:16; Heb 10:24–25; 2 Cor 5:17; Gal 5:22–24).

13. We know when we die as a Christian in an
    instant we will be transferred across the death
    line to a place we call heaven.

14. There we will dwell for all eternity glorifying
    and praising God as Father, Son, and Holy
    Spirit. We will have God's everlasting fellow-
    ship, mercy, physical joy, and spiritual joy
    (Dan 12:2; Matt 25:46; 1 Pet 1:3–5; Rev 7:9–17;
    Rev 21:1–27; Rev 22:1–5).

15. Now, the last question with three parts:
    "Where do you find yourself on this diagram?
    Which path are you on during your earthly
    journey? Where will you spend eternity?"
    When death takes away your time, your

existence after death will be in only one of two places.

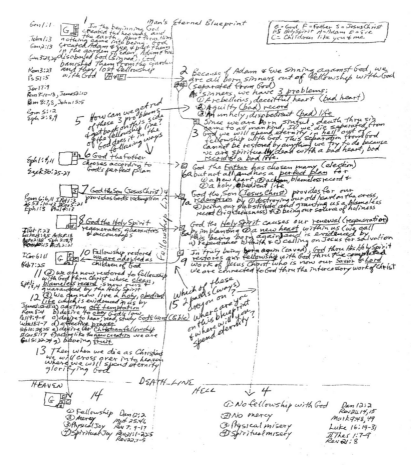

Man's Eternal Blueprint

Gen 1:1
In the beginning God
created the heavens and
John 1:3   the earth. Apart from Him
Gen 2:13   nothing came into being. God
Gen 3:23,24 created Adam & Eve & put them
             in the garden of Eden. Adam & Eve
Rom 3:23   disobeyed God (sinned). God
Ps 51:5   banished them from the garden
             and they lost fellowship
             with God

E = God   F = Father   S = Jesus Christ
HS Holy Spirit   A = Adam   E = Eve
C = Children like you & me

2 Because of Adam & Eve sinning against God, we
  are all born sinners out of fellowship with God
  (separated from God)

Jer 17:9
Rom 7:10-18, James 2:10   As sinners, we have 3 problems:
Rom 8:7,8, John 15:5   ① A rebellious, deceitful heart (bad heart)
                             ② A guilty (bad) record
Rom 5:12   ③ An unholy, disobedient (bad) life
Eph 2:8,9

5 How can we get rid
  of these 3 problems?   3 Since we are born sinful, death thru sin
  Is not both on this side   came to all mankind. If we die separated from
  of the fellowship line?   fellowship with God. This separation from God
  & not God does it in the   cannot be restored by anything we try to do because
  of God's following ways   we are spiritually dead with a bad heart, bad
                             record of a bad life.

Eph 1:4,11   6 God the Father
Ezek 36:25-27 chooses according to   6a God the Father has chosen many, (election)
               God's perfect plan   ① a new heart ② a perfect plan for
                                          ② a holy, obedient life & a blameless record &

Rom 6:6,11   7 God the Son (Jesus Christ) &   7a God the Son (Jesus Christ) provides for our
I Pet 1:3   provides God's redemption   redemption by ① destroying our old heart on the cross,
Is 53:10-12 2 Cor 5:21   ② being our substitute and granting us a blameless
Eph 1:13 Phil 4:13   record (righteousness) & ③ being our source of holiness

I Pet 1:23   8 God the Holy Spirit   8a God the Holy Spirit causes our renewal (regeneration)
Lk 24:13,15 Acts 4:18 regenerates, guarantees   by ① implanting ② a new heart within us (we call
Acts 2:38 Eph 2:8,9   & encourages   this being born again) and is evidenced by
Rom 8:13 Acts 2:21   a) repentance b) faith & c) calling on Jesus for salvation

I Cor 6:11   10 Fellowship restored   9 In truly being born again (saved), God thru His to Holy Spirit
Heb 7:25   we are adopted as   restores our fellowship with God thru the completed
               children of God   work of Jesus Christ who is now our Savior & Lord
                                        We are connected to God thru the intercessory work of Christ

             11 ② we are now restored to fellowship
Eph 1,4   with God thru Christ whose clean,
               blameless record is now ours &
               guaranteed by the Holy Spirit

             12 ③ We can now live a holy, obedient   Which of these
James 1:2-5 a) resting off temptation   2 paths (ways)
Rom 8:14 b) desire to obey (God's law)   are you on?
Ps 119:9-11 c) desire to hear, read, study God's word (Bible)   Where are you
Luke 18:1-7 d) effective prayer   on this blueprint
Heb 10:24,25 e) desire for Christian fellowship   & where will you
2 Cor 5:17 Bearing like the new creation we are   spend eternity?
Gal 5:22-24 g) bearing fruit

             13 Then when we die as Christians
                we will cross over into heaven
                where we will spend eternity
                glorifying God

HEAVEN   — DEATH LINE —   HELL   ↓ 4

14   ① No fellowship with God   Dan 12:2
① Fellowship Dan 12:2   ② No mercy   Rev 20:14,15
② Mercy Matt 25:46   ③ Physical misery   Matt 9:48, 49
③ Physical Joy Rev 7, 9-17   ④ Spiritual misery   Luke 16:19-31
④ Spiritual Joy Rev 21:1-22:5   II Thes 1:7-9
               Rev 22:1-5   Rev 21:8

If you are a Christian, you know the good news that death has been abolished and destroyed. God has provided a way for His chosen ones. Death cannot do anything, but we also know that death occurs for everyone until the Lord returns. (See 2 Samuel 14:14; 2 Timothy 1:8–10.)

As Christians we die the death of the righteous, knowing Jesus has conquered death. We know we go from this life to eternal life in an instant. Death is a shadow, and a shadow is not capable of harm. (See Numbers 23:10; Psalm 23:4; Luke 16:22.) So let's all be wise and careful how we live each day, sizing up and properly using our gifts at every opportunity. (See Ephesians 5:15 and Colossians 4:5.)

Your Will Be Done!

This appendix includes suggestions on how to handle some of the details my family and I managed before and after Gini's death. Although the Internet has information, I think it would be helpful to many of you that I provide this list and make some recommendations. Death takes time in the sense you can choose to take some of your own time to prepare in advance of your own death for the transfer of your earthly possessions to others, or that process will take more time from your heirs after your death. Either way, this is another aspect of how our death takes time.

Here I have generalized the aspects of things you can do during life outside of your directives in a will. But, I cannot overemphasize that you make sure you have a will. Lastly, I have listed some of the processes necessary for loved ones in the days and months after your death, in the process called probate. After you die, all traces of your identification and existence regarding ownership is fairly quickly removed. The following are my layman suggestions and not a legal opinion. Obtaining a legal and/or accounting opinion as to your specific needs is strongly encouraged. I offer the following based upon my own experiences and needs. And, one more thing: arrange for someone to be at your house during the visitation and funeral because burglars read obituaries and funeral notices to target empty homes.

General Suggestions during Your Lifetime outside of Your Will

Review and list details of all of your ownership in such things as house, car, boat, property, safe deposit box, stock accounts, and banking accounts. Generally these will be in the categories of needing a title or ownership and require signatures. Although there are exceptions where a tax or an estate legal opinion may suggest a different approach, generally you want to have joint ownership that is "or" and not "and," or joint title with right of survivorship. For banking- and stock-related matters, your bank or stock broker can help you with this process. If your family has corporate entities such as partnerships, corporations, or LLCs, you need to make sure the corporate documents have a section that determines the distribution of assets upon the death of a member, unit holder, or stockholder.

Your legal counsel may also have suggestions for other directives for you to make that may help your heirs be able to completely avoid the probate process explained below. It may be advantageous in some instances to have property or accounts in only one spouse's name, and if he or she is the first spouse to die, then expert help from an estate lawyer and/or accountant will probably be necessary. As an example, if securities were held in only the deceased's name, there may be a step up in what is called the basis (the original amount paid for the security). This means the value at date of death will be the new base value and thus may avoid some capital gains taxes.

I cannot emphasize too strongly to have a listing of all assets, including account numbers, passwords, descriptions, and individuals to contact, as well as a listing of household items including any directives as to whom you might suggest they be given to upon your death (especially helpful are written notes of any history of inherited or keepsake items). In our case, my wife only made suggestions in her directives and left the final decision to our children and myself as to the exact division of her assets.

Make sure there is a conversation about the desires of all family members when they become sick or disabled and cannot make medical decisions on their own. This can be informal or be official in the form of a living will, health care power of attorney, or a letter of instruction. Make sure someone knows where these and other documents are kept.

I strongly suggest you have a medical directive or medical power of attorney completed for your spouse and you. In case a spouse is unable to understand, make decisions, talk, or write—or incapable in some other way—it may also be a good idea to have, and then be able to make active, a general or durable power of attorney, as it allows the spouse to make all decisions for the other, except for changes in the will. This power of attorney will allow you to continue to use joint checking accounts and pay credit cards or other expenses, not only during the incapacitated life of your spouse but also in the immediate time period after death.

Obtaining a cemetery plot or a directive as to how you wish your remains to be handled is quite helpful to the survivors. If possible you should obtain the grave marker or stone already completed and arrange the specifics of such things as your casket, your desired Scripture and songs, or anything else in your funeral service. Go ahead and write out your obituary specifics to include next of kin full names and memorial designation. This is so helpful to your family in releasing a major burden and their time in the immediate grieving period.

A Will

I have always been amazed at how many people do not have a will. They can be quite simple and only require minimal legal help and expertise in the vast majority of cases. Although some people need to have a fairly complex will to accomplish what they desire to do, most of us can have a straightforward, short will. For my wife and me, our wills did not have a specific section about what items went to whom. Instead, we had a separate guidance document for only our heirs to know about. This way we did not have to constantly be changing the will to be able to change the worldly goods we added and subtracted, including moving houses, selling a piece of property, losing a wedding ring, and similar things. With my wife's cancer diagnosis, we also had changes in our cash and securities accounts we did not have to worry about.

Make sure you know where the original copy of the will is kept. If it is in a safe deposit box, make sure the box is in two names with separate individual access allowed, or the box will be barred from access, which can make things quite complicated!

Probate: the After-Death Process

When someone dies, many things change. First, there is a death certificate, followed by instructions that you need to go to the Probate Court within a month of the death with a copy of the death certificate, will, and other needed documents. Call them first to see if they require any other items (if there is no will, then the Probate judge considers the intestate [without will] process and assigns an executor). After a review, the executor and trustee of your will must accomplish a list of items in the next several months. The process can provide for temporary completion in as little as three months, but the earliest permanent closing of the estate is usually nine months. I am going to list the most common items necessary to complete, but in some estates, there are additional items (and some may have to be handled by an expert attorney in estate matters). Only a few of these will be necessary to complete the official probate requirements in most estates.

1. If there is a will, the executor of the will should file as soon as possible with the Probate Court (if no will, consult with the Probate Court for directions). About a week after the death, call them as to what you need to bring, but at a minimum you will need the death certificate and the original will, as well as the addresses of persons named in the will. They will keep the will and make a copy for you to keep. By the way, if there is no property or assets in the deceased's name, there is no need to go to probate, but they can be quite helpful.

2. The Probate Court will give you copies of a Certificate of Appointment (as personal representative for the estate), which allows you to make decisions and transactions on behalf of the estate.

3. In most cases, they will provide you with an accounting and recording sheet for any items you complete.

4. The probate process will first submit a notice of death in the newspaper that allows you to notify anyone with outstanding debts of their need to collect from the estate of the deceased and file a request with the court. The time period can vary but is usually not closed until

nine months after the notice is printed. This notification is still required in the event probate is not needed.

5. The executor, now called personal representative, will then be instructed on how to inform all heirs listed in the will.

6. You will be required to submit a paid-in-full receipt for funeral expenses.

7. The Probate Court will review the items in the will that require a report to them, and then everything else is outside of probate.

8. You will be given a list of items and tasks to complete and return to the court in a timely manner.

9. You will need quite a few original copies of the death certificate, and the funeral home usually gives you at least six to ten copies.

10. Now you begin the process of notifying and canceling. I suggest the first be the Social Security office where you take a copy of your Certificate of Appointment and a copy of the original death certificate, wait in line, and then apply for the death benefit and any other benefits you may qualify for. They will also help to cancel any payments being made on behalf of the deceased or change any future payment amounts. If the deceased receives a monthly

benefit, it stops the month before the month of death, so there may even be a refund due of the current month payment that will be removed from your bank account. If the surviving spouse is the lower wage earner, an increase in benefits may be paid to the survivor. If you also have other deductions being made, such as Medicare A and B or drug plan payments, they will cancel for you. Going to the Social Security office is also important to make sure that the deceased has been entered into the Social Security Master Death Index. This prevents fraudulent collecting of a dead person's Social Security payments or attempts to open a credit account in the deceased's name.

11. Call the health insurance plan the deceased was enrolled in and have them cancel the policy, which may require your submitting documentation. If there is a Medicare supplement insurance plan, they usually can check with the Social Security records, and that will be sufficient for them to cancel—similarly for any other care policies such as for long-term care.

12. Call your insurance company for your home, car, boat, liability, and any other insurance, and they will instruct you as to what needs to

be done to remove the deceased's name from the insurance policies.

13. Call any life insurance companies if there are policies and submit any required documents. Life insurance payments are usually outside of probate, and you will also receive a prorated refund of the premium paid for the current period. You may need to consult an accountant or estate attorney to determine if any tax is due on insurance proceeds.

14. Notify your bank, trusts, security firms, and safe deposit box (hopefully you have already gone and removed any safe deposit items so an accounting of those items is not necessary). In some cases, only a simple change of name on the account is required, and in other instances, the process calls for more documentation.

15. Cancel credit cards solely in the name of the deceased. In most instances, you call the number on the back of the card and talk with a representative about what needs to be done. In some instances, if you have the username and password for Internet access to the account, you can simply send a secure message asking that the credit card be closed with no further explanation. In the majority of cases,

this will be successful and save considerable time. This is also a good time to review past statements for any recurrent charges that either need to be cancelled or transferred to another form of payment.

16. Send a letter with a copy of the death certificate to each of the three major credit bureaus to request they list on their credit report: "Deceased – Do not issue credit." Include your name, address, relationship to the deceased, and ask for a copy of the updated credit report reflecting the changes requested.

17. Notify any employer, as there may be spousal or other survivor benefits available.

18. Notify the Veterans Administration if the deceased was a veteran. Often the funeral home can help with this as there may be some funeral expense benefits.

19. Check with any other organizations the deceased belonged to if there is a benefit available.

20. Cancel cell phones, memberships, and subscriptions. Review the last year of credit card statements to identify any recurrent charges. Cancel any standing orders for one-time or recurring delivery (this might include care items, prescription drugs, or an unneeded

Internet order). Cancel any social media accounts such as Facebook, Twitter, Snapchat, and Instagram.

21. If the deceased had debts due from someone, contact that person or entity for collection of the debt.

22. As appropriate, cancel or make name changes on all utility accounts. If no one is continuing to live at the deceased's address, notify the USPS of address change and have mail for the deceased delivered to an appropriate address.

23. Obtain help from a lawyer and/or accountant with the filing of taxes for the year in which death occurred to make sure all the forms are properly completed and filed. In some cases an additional estate income tax form 1041 may be required, whether or not any tax is due, as the dollar amounts of the estate affect the surviving spouse's future estate details. For some larger estates, form 706 may need to be completed. Obtain the help of an estate lawyer and an accountant as the IRS audits 100 percent of these submissions.

24. The 706 process with the federal government may be necessary to preserve any unused portion of the death exemption to pass on to the surviving spouse. It is not often needed

but for larger estates is a necessity. Currently (in 2016) the exemption is about $5.6 million. Nearly always, at least a portion of the assets of the deceased go to the surviving spouse, so this then means that any exemption amount that is unused can be transferred to the surviving spouse. When the surviving spouse dies, his or her death exemption for federal estate taxes can then include the unused portion. Otherwise, the surviving spouse is limited to the then current amount for an individual, even though assets were received because of the spouse's death. Although the current amount seems generous, just a few years ago the amount was only $1 million for each individual. An act of congress can change the amount allowed, but it currently has a built-in inflation rise each year. Please note that you will have to have a knowledgeable accountant help you with this form as it is a bit complicated and there is a 100 percent review by the federal government, so careful documentation of each item included in the report is necessary.

25. The estate plan and will of the surviving spouse should be reviewed to make any necessary revisions.

About the Author

Dr. Gene Baillie grew up in rural Nebraska, the oldest of six children and the first member of his family to attend college. He and Gini were married during his first year of medical school. Pathology training and two years of public health service came after medical school, and Gene practiced pathology for thirty-five years in Anderson, South Carolina.

For many years, he taught technologist and pathology courses at a national level, and he was elected to the board of the American Society for Clinical Pathology, serving as their president in 2002–2003. He has written several medical articles, including one with his daughter Becky about biblical leprosy.

Gene and Gini raised three biological children—Becky, Kim, and Heather—who are now married and have blessed Gene and Gini with eight grandchildren. The Baillies also raised four foster sons who were part of a family of eight children.

All eight children are considered part of the Baillie family, as are their children. The Baillie family includes many spiritual children and grandchildren as well. Gene and Gini were blessed to travel on mission trips to Korea, Taiwan, Japan, Jamaica, Republic of Congo, and Liberia. They also were a part of planting four churches, including one in Australia, where Gene worked for five years teaching pathology to medical doctors.

He is an elder in the Presbyterian Church in America. Over the years, the Baillie home served as a site for newly started churches and as a place for Gene and Gini to teach inductive Bible studies. For more than a quarter of a century, Gene has been passionate about reading the Bible through each year and he has encouraged many others, by weekly accountability, to do the same.

Dr Baillie has written two other books. *The Journey Home* is about walking through and rising above times of hardship and pain during the trials the Lord allows in our lives. The book is also a love story of fifty years of marriage and devotion to one another, seeing the Lord as the I AM all sufficient for every need. To order or watch the video on marriage vows, go to www .ReadTheJourneyHome.com.

The other book is *Nothing Matters* concerning a glibly used word pervasive in culture, the world, and in the Bible. Nothing is really something and does matter! That *nothing* has significance. "You enter the world with nothing, and it is certain you will leave with nothing" (see 1 Timothy 6:7). What is that nothing? Learn more at www.ReadNothing Matters.com.

Visit www.DeathTakesTime.com or www .ReadGoodBooks.org to order additional copies. If you desire to contact the author, please send your message to GeneBaillie@gmail.com.

Endnotes

1. C. S. Lewis, *A Grief Observed* (New York: HarperOne, 2009).

2. Albert Einstein, *News Chronicle*, March 14, 1949.

3. D. L. Moody, sermon, Moody Bible Church, Chicago.

4. J. R. R. Tolkien, *The Fellowship of the Ring* (London: George Allen and Unwin, 1954).

5. Nancy Guthrie, ed., *O Love That Will Not Let Me Go: Facing Death with Courageous Confidence in God* (Wheaton, IL: Crossway, 2011), 79–86.

6. *Forrest Gump*, 1994; Paramount Pictures, a Steve Tisch/Wendy Finerman Production, a Robert Zemeckis Film.

CPSIA information can be obtained
at www.ICGtesting.com
Printed in the USA
FSOW04n0641130516
20303FS